The

# ROB ROY ON THE BALTIC:

## 𝔄 Canoe Cruise,
THROUGH
## NORWAY, SWEDEN, DENMARK, SLESWIG HOLSTEIN, THE NORTH SEA, AND THE BALTIC

BY
## J. MACGREGOR, M.A.,
TRINITY COLLEGE, CAMBRIDGE,
AUTHOR OF "A THOUSAND MILES IN THE ROB ROY CANOE," FIFTEENTH
EDITION;
"THE ROB ROY ON THE JORDAN," ETC.

*With numerous Illustrations, Maps, and Music*

*Dixon-Price Publishing*
Kingston, Washington

Library of Congress Cataloging-in-Publication Data

MacGregor, John, 1825-1892.
 The Rob Roy on the Baltic : a canoe cruise through Norway, Sweden, Denmark, Sleswig Holstein, the North Sea, and the Baltic / by J. MacGregor ; with numerous illustrations, maps, and music.
     p. cm.
 Originally published: 10th ed. London, England : Sampson Low, Marston & Co., 1894.
 ISBN-13: 978-1-929516-20-9
 ISBN-10: 1-929516-20-7
 1. MacGregor, John, 1825-1892--Travel--Europe, Northern. 2. Rob Roy (Yawl) 3. Europe, Northern--Description and travel. 4. Scandinavia--Description and travel. 5. Schleswig-Holstein (Germany)--Description and travel. 6. Baltic Sea--Description and travel. 7. North Sea--Description and travel. 8. Canoes and canoeing--Europe, Northern--History--19th century. 9. Canoes and canoeing--North Sea--History--19th century. 10. Canoes and canoeing--Baltic Sea--History--19th century. I. Title.
 DL9.M14 2009
 914.804'5--dc22

                    2008056098


ISBN-10: 1-929516-20-7
ISBN-13: 978-1-929516-20-9

*Dixon-Price Publishing*
Kingston, Washington

# PREFACE

QUITE new things will meet us in this cruise, and different from those we told of in the former voyage.

Then we had the rapids to shoot, and shallows to wade, and Swiss glaciers and German castles and French omelettes to discuss.

Now we have to dash into salt water, to sail over inland seas, to grope amid foggy islands, and to fish and to cook under lonely, gaunt rocks.

Which cruise was the better one it is not easy to say. Each of then had its log; and the chips from one are not like the shavings from the other—except in this, that they come from a pleasant paddle.

JOHN MACGREGOR

TEMPLE, *London*, 1872

# CONTENTS

# ILLUSTRATIONS, MAPS, &c.

# CHAPTER I.

THE first cruise of the "Rob Roy" was a most charming voyage through Belgium, Prussia, and Bavaria, by the Meuse and the Rhine, the Main and the Danube, then among the lakes of Switzerland, and on the Aar and the Reuss, and returning through France over the Vosges Mountains, and then by the Moselle, the Meurthe, the Marne, and the Seine.

After people had read the account of the cruise, other canoes were speedily built; the Canoe Club was formed. The Prince of Wales became our Commodore, and the Prince Imperial joined and paddled a Rob Roy.

It was so very pleasant to travel in the old canoe that I ventured out on a second cruise, and now we shall have its log.

The hard-won experience of the former voyage was a great advantage to the canoeist; and perhaps the reader, too, has read what was written about it.[1]

So we are going together, you and I, as old hands and old friends, but to new lands and on fresh waters, and in a beautiful new boat built with every excellence that the "Rob Roy" had, and a hundred more.

This new canoe had been carefully designed in the winter, after numerous experiments in other boats.[2]

She is shorter, narrower, shallower, lighter, and stronger than the old "Rob Roy," and yet she is built to sail on wider lakes, and to cross green seas, and to live in wilder places than were tried thus before. Therefore, also, we find in her a little basket with cooking things, and rice, soup, tea, coffee, chocolate, sugar, salt, and a good supply of biscuits, so that, with these provisions, we can stop where there is no house to rest at, and can dine on a lonely islet, lighting a great log fire, which will smoke away for an hour or two after we are gone, and we can look back upon its cloud-wreaths curling for miles behind us. The caboose of the "Rob Roy" has also a spirit furnace; and the whole affair in the basket weighs about 3 lbs., while my luggage for three months' cruising weighs 9 lbs., and is carried in the same black bag which was used before, being one foot square in size, by five inches deep. Moreover, a small packet of "reserve stores" is sent on a fortnight in advance, with more eatables and maps and books in it, for body and mind sha'n't starve.

A week's trial of the "Rob Roy" (the new boat is now meant when we use this name)[3] showed that every alteration made is an improvement. The paddle, so light as to weigh only 2½ pounds, is supremely handy. The sails fitted admirably (after eight sets had been made). The arched deck, ridiculed by many when it was proposed, is now admitted to be grace itself; and so the fishing-rod is slung on its india-rubber band, and the canoe is pronounced complete.

The excellent grey flannel suit that had been worn for months, and rubbed and scrubbed and drenched and wrung some scores of times last year, was mustered for inspection, and as no button was absent and no seam was loose, this ancient uniform[4] was ordered again for foreign service, and a fresh straw hat was enrolled. New plans had been devised for the luggage bag, but they were all inferior to the old one, which thus triumphantly again secured its berth aboard, though in a better part of the ship—that is, ahead of the stretcher—and so more conveniently stowed out of the way.

The hair-brush is the same, and the new comb is a bit of the old one. A new drawing book, and the No. 2 trousers, and the same little Testament, found alongside them now a warmer Sunday coat and a wonderful woven vest (to replace the one stolen on the Rhine), and which can be worn over everything or under all—an important capacity when you change from hot paddling to cooler sailing many times in a day.

Then the shape and weight and size of every minute article of the outfit had to be studiously arranged; they must be fitted together like the words in hexameter verse; and the time and thought spent in this equipment were well repaid by a most successful voyage in safety and comfort, with the least possible expenditure of muscle and trouble by the way.

And now as to victualling the ship—a new department. It was great fun to settle about this, and a practical lesson as to "what to eat, drink, and avoid." How many inches of portable soup may we load on board, and how many ounces of rice, squares of chocolate, cups of coffee-essence, and spoonsful of tea—all to be brought from London, for these things are best had there.

The medicine-chest is the same as before (a match-box holds it all), but quinine was added for the aguish lakes.

Then there were the "ship's stores" in a pillbox, and the "tailor's shop" for the crew—one spare button, and one threaded needle in a cork, guarded by twelve pins.

Maps—excellent ones—were duly chopped up into squares for pocket use, and a lens was added, to read them by in dusky twilight. Lastly, the foot of magnesium wire left over from last year was put on board, together with "the collar." Only the wading shoes were discarded; for now we are to rock on deeper waves, and a phial of brandy will be more useful than canvas slippers, and a life-preserver, of cork, nine inches square, will serve to float the crew a little when the ship goes down "all standing."

Two articles only were failures; the rope for a painter, though chosen with infinite care from the "Alpine Club" cords, never would keep soft when it was wet; and the captain's new metal-hafted knife, ferretted out from a Bond Street shop, at fifteen shillings, snapped, blade after blade, in a week, until it was replaced by a good, rough, honest-looking Swedish knife at five shillings, which lasted to the end.

We have not half done yet with the list of things; but you may think the canoe really must now be ready to start. No, there is the live stock, i.e., the ship's dog. Chosen for me by the best dog man in the world, little "Rob" was the very best dog in the universe. Light, plucky, pleasant, and aqueous, not at all pretty, but admirably good. The scholar saw him in his proper place as the "second person singular of *cano;*" and to others, ignorant even of dog Latin, he would say in plain English, "My bark is on the wave."

He would sit on the deck behind me, and in the funniest way used to—well, never mind, now—he was stolen just before I started; and very likely he would have been often a pleasure, and very often a bore.[5]

As our steamer from London, on the 2nd of August, nears the town of Christiania, which sits like a queen on the fjord, in bright colours and graceful outlines, the sight ought to be seen by all the passengers, but we have some new travellers on board, who select just this particular half hour for packing up their things in the dim and fusty cabin. After all the pretty scenery has been passed (and they have come precisely to see this), one of them emerges on deck in overpowering knickerbockers, brilliant red stockings, and polished pumps. How the natives will stare when he lands! But let us draw a veil over those ruby legs, for every traveller must once be young; the best of us have to enter the long lane of touring by the green end.

The quay is reached, and the Rob Roy is now aroused

from its two days' sleep in the steamer's life-boat during our voyage, and the first crowd of gazers on shore follows the canoe to the railway.

The travellers' friend in Norway is Mr. Bennet, who knows everything and helps everybody. He fills several posts of duty and honour, has an office full of maps and books, and a yard full of carrioles and carriages, and a desk full of outlandish bank notes for shillings; and, if you wish to journey safe and fast over Norway, and with big fish to the rod, and big bags to the gun, it is well to talk first with Mr. Bennet. He had aided me there ten years ago; but now it was an utterly new line to be catechized upon by the first English traveller mad about boats, and so he was fairly nonplussed. In short, there was no reliable information to be had for a canoe journey, and thus there was all the pleasure to be felt in a voyage of discovery.

People in the town were soon interested, however, about the little skiff, in proportion to their own intelligence and appreciation of the novelty of the enterprise; and specially the railway engineers, who (as well as those on steamers) are ever the friends of the paddler.

Any one can see by the map that Norway and Sweden are covered with an entanglement of water in rivers, lakes, and pools, netted together all over the broad surface for a thousand miles, and we have resolved to push our way through these seas and streams somehow or other, right away to Stockholm.[6]

After duly considering the pros and cons of five different routes, the line I selected required me to take the canoe to Kongsvinger, which is north-east of Christiania about sixty miles. The railway to this runs alongside the lovely Glommen River, which winds and winds and eddies and glides just as the Rhine does about Waldshut, and is almost as full of water and as pretty. There was a natural curiosity in my peeps out of the carriage window to see the rapids and whirlpools we might possibly have to rush down or spin round in here; but it has been found that a private rehearsal of this sort does little good; for when you are in a boat, and on the water, it is impossible to remember how any place looked from the railway train, so as to obtain real benefit from the remembrance.

But we are to leave the Glommen, and the Rob Roy

must go modestly on a far humbler water; so next morning she is placed in a *dresine*, a carriage on the railway moved by cranks and treadles for the feet, as a velocipede is worked, and to which vehicle there clung as many persons as could hold by it, while we rumbled along until a halt was made near the shore of a small lake, from which the water overflows in winter into the Glommen, and so to the Skaggerak, while its only ordinary fall is south-east by a long and winding route into the all-absorbing Vener See, and so into the Kattegat.

When the Rob Roy was carried over the rank grass, and gently launched on this wild water, and the visitors stood alongside pleasantly smiling, and the first stroke of the paddle moved new ripples on its virgin bosom, then there came into my soul a thrill of pleasure. "Once more free, alone, exploring—all before me now is unknown and untried, but sure to be jolly." If in such a time a man is not elated, he cannot, I think, be the right man for a canoe.

The Rob Roy's engine soon settled down to work with a regular swing; and the even strokes of the dark-blue blades were long and strong in the new water. Then the mind, placid in solitude, turned itself inwards, thinking of the length of the journey—the possible perils of the enterprise—the unknown difficulties to be met, the mysterious future of incidents to happen, the strange people and queer languages, and curious nights and days, the falls and deeps, the rapids and shallows, the waves and whirlpools, the upsets and groundings, the calms and breezes. These and all the other countless varied features of a lonely water journey in a foreign land were all imagined with an eager, intense longing to meet them every one.

What did happen afterwards on this very day might well have turned me back at once ; but now it is well that we went on through it all, else I should have lost one of the happiest seasons in my life, one of the best of my journeys abroad.

## END NOTES

1—A Thousand Miles in the Rob Roy Canoe on Lakes and Rivers of Europe. With 20 Illustrations and a Map. Eighth edition. 1871. Low and Marston. Among the private laudations of the volume must be cited with applause the mot of an eccentric man, who was asked if he had read the "Canoe Book," and replied with animation, "Of course ; it's not half so good as 'Ecce Homo.'"

2—The incessant changes and countermands of her anxious designer in search of perfection worried the builders; and it is said that, while the new canoe was being made, Mr. Searle "suffered much from Rob Roy on the brain." A full description of the new "Rob Roy" will be found in the Appendix.

3—The old original Rob Roy made several trips in England after her "thousand miles" abroad, and then she was taken in the "Sappho" yacht, with with the "Rollo" canoe, of similar build, for a cruise along the coast of Norway; and the little twin skiffs paddled and sailed among the northern fjords, and at last round the North Cape itself, returning to England safe, but battered and travel worn. The old "Mother Rob Roy" now rests at Searle's. The new canoe being shown at the Paris Exhibition caused the Prince Imperial of France to join the Canoe Club.

4—It will not be a breach of confidence to say that this Norfolk jacket was made by Meyer and Mortimer of Conduit Street.

5—Another 'Rob' in my cruise of 1871 was killed by a steamer at night in the Zuider Zee.

6—See Map 2.

# CHAPTER II.

Too fast — Oklangen Lake — Refractory Rice — Tracts —
Papier Maché — A Thought or Two — Old Lady No. 1 —
Dark Music — Behind the Scenes — Mamma and Daughter
— Rapids of the Vrangs.

AT the end of the quiet lake, wooded thickly to its edge,
the map showed a river; but, alas! no river was there; and as
I wondered in silence, the quiet woods suddenly resounded
with the blast of a trumpet. In a deep sequestered nook
there were three companies of men drilling amid the
trees—the very last thing one would expect to meet as the
first event of a voyage. Every man of them caught sight of
the Rob Roy, and they marched on, indeed, in column, but
all had "Eyes right," for they were all staring sideways at
the canoe.

This military and naval combination was not in their
"Red Book;" so the officer, being a wise man, dismissed his
array, and down they rushed *en masse* to the water.

The officer, Captain Venson, explained to me in French,
that they were the local Landvehr, camping out for six days;
and as the men crowded round, each holding his hat in his
hand whenever he came within a certain radius of his
captain's august presence, and caressing the little canoe
with smiles of pleasure, he posted a sentry with fixed
bayonet to guard the Rob Roy, lying on the green rushes in
the sun; and he led me off to his hut, so prettily garnished
with nasturtiums and pictures—one of them a print labelled

"View of Hackney Church," at least a hundred years old. Then, after refreshments served, a cart was got, and we started for another lake. The soldier leading the horse allowed it to go too fast, and in vain I shouted to stop. All the others shouted too. Off started the spirited nag down hill, and dragging the man after him, until the pace quickened into a full gallop; and the more we shouted the worse it was, for the horse kicked and plunged, and overthrew the man, and then darted into a corn-field, and headlong rushed down to a gate, where the cart was dashed to pieces, the wheels going one way, and the horse and shafts and canoe dragged along at a racing pace, till at another fence the whole was overturned, amid a crash of broken palings.

All this occurred in about as much time as you will take to read the account, but this time was enough to let me—running at full speed—become cheerfully resigned to the terrible catastrophe, and even to arrive on the scene with a laugh (hysteric probably), and the thought, "Well, it is sad; but it is better the poor little boat should be entirely smashed rather than have only some deadly wounds, and so need to be helped along limping for months in a lingering existence of leaks and patches."

I heeded not the broken cart and the runaway horse, but rushed to my canoe. I turned her over as one would tenderly handle a child thrown from a carriage, and what was my wonder to find she was perfectly whole—only the flagstaff broken, and one or two ribs, and scarcely a scratch on the fine varnish, and not one crack in the cedar deck. Nay, there was not a bottle smashed in my stores, and all this because she had made a somersault on the paling just broken, as she landed on it most happily on her strong oak stem, which still bears a deep mark, but no other injury.

This adventure was so extraordinary, and the escape so marvellous, that we have detailed it at length, and do earnestly hope we shall never have to recount another of the kind.[1]

The officer positively refused to let me pay for the ruined cart, saying it belonged to the "subsidy," and he was proud to help me. He was in earnest, too, and it was but an augury of many like acts of Scandinavian love of the Englishman.

A new cart took us to Oklangen Lake, deep and dark, with matted trees and luxuriant plants overgrowing its rocky sides. After a delightful paddle along this I was most glad to find no water in the hold—not a nail had been started. Let every canoeist abide by my advice to have an oak canoe.

The roar of a waterfall told that the river was now available; so we have fairly begun the Vrangs Elv at its very source. A large saw-mill was here, but not a man was to be seen: they had all gone to dinner (*i middags*); so we thought it would be a good idea to do the same. We dragged the Rob Roy to the "smithy," and rigged up our fire on the anvil, fencing it round with bricks to keep the draught from the little lamp. Preserved soup was soon boiling with a savoury

odour, and we put lots of rice in, but somehow the grains of rice would not get large, as you have them when properly cooked, and we soon found they ought to be steeped first. However, there was no time for a hungry man to wait, so, large or small, the rice was capital to eat with my wooden spoon and fork (they are united in one), and with biscuits and mild brandy-and-water the bivouac was done.

The workpeople were astonished on their return to find the anvil with a banquet on it; and when all was packed up we launched on the river again, which for some miles was like a little Scotch trout stream, with purling ripples and long pools quite concealed by thick foliage, tangled ferns, and fallen larches, drooping so low as to cause me to stoop again and again to pass. Sometimes I had to wade again and again to pass. Sometimes I had to wade, but the fine summer-day sun made this pleasant, and it was cool to dabble in the bright crystal stream, and chase the water ousels or grasp at the fish, always, however, in vain.

In travelling abroad where you cannot speak fluently their language, and yet you pass among thousands of men and women who are on life's road with yourself, and who would hear a friendly word about another life, if you could speak to them on this great subject, it is very well that you can give them on paper, and in their own tongue plainly printed, what is good for them and for you to think of every day.

Because many tracts are weak and badly written, and are given imprudently, therefore some people decry all tracts. Because papers are given somewhere unwisely they would have you give no papers abroad. It would be quite as logical to denounce all talk with the foreigners, because a good deal of talk is most vapid. The Norwegians and Swedes are able to read. More of them are so far educated than in the like number of any nation of Europe. They eagerly accept papers (call them tracts, or not), and they do this more readily from Englishmen, and most readily when the man who gives them is otherwise enlisting their attention by his manner of life or travel. No place, therefore, is better suited for giving tracts than Scandinavia.

The following story will show, however, that good tracts must be rightly carried as well as prudently given. In a former journey here three of us brought 3000 tracts and many Testaments for distribution. A great bundle of these was packed in the same tin case with some pounds of hard biscuits, and this was placed on my carriole. The rattling made by this incongruous packet attracted my attention when we first set off and jolted along; but I noticed that the sound got more and more dead after some miles on the road, until at last it subsided into a deep-toned thump as the wheels went over a stone.

At night we opened the tin box, and found only a mass of fine dust like meal. The biscuits were pounded into grains, and little bits of paper, with one letter perhaps on each, represented the luckless tracts that had been packed with them.

But what remained in other bundles of our papers and books were given and received with pleasure among thousands. People ran along the road to beg for a paper, and often it was handed to them on the end of a whip. Sometimes these were read among crowds of attentive listeners; at other times boats came to us on lakes by moonlight or by the Aurora gleams, and entreated they might have a "bok," offering us money for a New Testament.

As to the amount of good these tracts may do, let those speak (yes, and *only* those) who have carefully given them, and patiently watched the results. For my own part, after many years' experience in the matter, I am fully convinced of the vast benefit done in this way, while fully sensible also of the need of prudence and common sense in using this means of good. And what means is there that does not require attentive regard in applying it, and prayer for a blessing on its use?

To ridicule the general practice of tract giving is too ridiculous. To put it down by banter is impossible; and you are not likely to improve it by laughing. Therefore let me say, once for all, that on this voyage, as on every other tour, I constantly gave tracts; feeling, too, that if the people around me were not available for this sort of communication, or if I was not ready to use it on their behalf, there must be some constraint on their side or on mine, which ought not to exist between the sons and daughters of Adam, pilgrims in a world together, and with great and broad and deep and lofty things in common, that ought never to be very distant from our thoughts, and which one day must be near. Now you have had a tract from the "Chaplain of the Canoe."

Another lake came next, and with it new pleasures; for there is as much difference between canoeing on rivers and lakes as there is between traversing mountains and plains. On the stream you have the current, the waterfall, the rapid, and the unfolding panorama, of which only a few hundred yards are seen at once. The lake, again, has its grander distances, its lofty cliffs, its rocks and islets, its stately trees, and its lively waves, which give quite another spirit to the boat, or if it is calm, then the weird picture on the liquid mirror shines back the sunlight at evening, and the floating clouds piled high in the air above are hugely massed again in reflection below.

But these clouds are not always so romantic and so far out of reach. Soon they closed round, and very prosaic rain teemed forth and hissed again on the surface of the lake. There was no eluding this straight downpour, and the crew might have mutinied had we gone on much longer in a deluge; so it was determined to stop at the only house, and to fish in the evening, if the rain should cease.

I put the Rob Roy safe under a bank, and walked through thick bushes to the humble dwelling. Only an old woman was inside—all the men were away; but we praised the scones she was baking, so she brought them in with coffee, but was evidently uncertain whether it might not all be a dream to see, for the very first time in her life, a grown man dressed in grey flannel, and talking what sounded to her like gibberish, yet manifestly very well able to eat like the mortals of her acquaintance.

Most luckily I managed to find two men on the road, and though they were wet and weary, mere tramps going on their way, they came with me to the boat, hidden under a bramble bush, with all the cows staring at it, as they always do here—indeed they will run along the bank of a river for half a mile with tails in the air, and "mooing" as fiercely as they can.

The worthy old dame was persuaded by signs to give me a room, and the men went off, after shaking hands vigorously, for sixpence each, and I coolly pulled the canoe right into this bedroom, if "bed" indeed it can be called, which was only straw, though the lady gave me a sheepskin—and a great population in it—to sleep upon, with my cork seat and macintosh for a pillow. Madame also brought in at night some *gröd* (porridge) and milk, a luxury not to be had in a hotel; so all four meals to-day were breakfasts. One chair was in the room, and two square blocks of timber; while green bushes with leaves on adorned the walls, and were sweet preserves for the mosquito game. The worst was she had no light of any kind; and to sit in the dark for hours before bedtime, with no one to speak to, and all one's thinking already exhausted in the boat, was a pretty start for the night. However, a light was found at eleven p.m., after hours of dark if not gloomy meditation, and just at the era when a squalling baby piped up for its nocturnal concerto.

For one so very fond of little children, it is but fair to hear them in their bad times, and not only in their good times. It would have been easy enough, then, to get on with the baby music; but a long and sad experience has made me acquainted with the tactics of the other minor visitors which now in a regular army marched to the attack from their camp in the sheepskin.

As a general maxim it is best, if there be only two or three of such intruders, to let them have their way, and they will go to sleep after a good supper, and then the victim may sleep too. But with hundreds and thousands this will not do. Put your trousers inside your stockings, tie your handkerchief over your face (making a hole for mouth and nose), stick your hands deep in your pockets, and if you can get asleep before the enemy finds his way into your entrenchment it is well. But if *one* light skirmisher gets in before you are fast asleep, be sure the army is not far behind. Your defences are enfiladed, and your flank is turned. You may now surrender, for that night is gone.

People are astir early in these parts. By five o'clock the household is on the move, and so am I; no toilet to make, no glass wherein to see.

"ONE'S BACK HAIR."

Behold how the neighbours have come in relays of six at a time. But none brings a basin, and so we must trust for a bath in the lake, calling to mind how, in this unkempt manner, once before, long ago, in a rough part of Norway, three of us went out to bathe, each clad only in a Scotch plaid; and as we stooped by a river and each used his tooth-brush, the populace assembled to learn and to admire.

After the exhibition had closed, and boiled eggs had been administered to the captain, and a scrubbing to the boat, we gave our hostess two shillings, which she said was far too much, though for three meals and a night's unrest surely it was moderate payment. Gratitude made her insist upon carrying the canoe herself to the water; so, with her daughter bearing the bow and mamma carrying the stern, the procession of three persons emerged from her door, and much laughter followed.

Oh the fresh air of the morning, with a new sun and another day, and all so still but the soft dip of the blue-bladed oar. Fat and fierce dragon-flies hover about me with their big staring eyes, and that little spider has fallen on the deck as it grazed the reeds just now. He walked all round, poor fellow, in vain seeking an escape, and dropping down a dozen times into the water, but always hauling up when that exit was found barred. He paused then, and seemed to ponder, and lifted his arm to the air to find if the wind would hoist him in a balloon of his own make. Think what an addition it would be to our capacities if we could at all times spin a hundred yards of fine rope strong enough to bear 200 lbs. weight! Has not that line of Terence—"Homo sum," &c.—the defect of excluding animals from our interest? Well, the cabin boy of the canoe became so concerned about our spider friend that at length we were constrained to pull to land that the pigmy spinner might be safe ashore.

After several lakes were traversed, with thick trees all round, and man, beast, and house entirely away, we got into full swing upon the river again, and for two days it twisted and turned amid rocks, green mossy banks, and thickets; always going fast enough to let me fish comfortably, and yet make progress all the time. We met only one serious rapid, or "force," as it is called, at Enteraden, and about fifty people gathered to see us pass over it. The caution which arises from experience made me somehow less daring about these rapids than in last year's voyage, feeling, perhaps, more now than ever before how much would be lost if a grand tour were to be cut short by smashing the canoe.

END NOTES
1—See Frontispiece.

# CHAPTER III.

Natives — How do you find the Way? — Which is it? — Water-logged — Wood, Wood — Dragging — Soft Men — Man in the Moon — Sleep-walker.

THE most frequent questions of inquiring visitors, when they send in their cards for a call on the Rob Roy, are the following:

"But how did you manage ahout the language?"

"And how did you find your way?"

To the first of these a reply at some length may be found in the account of my former tour, where the crew of the boat had to converse with people of four different languages, besides half-a-dozen *patois* and pure "bargee." In this northern expedition, also, we had to talk with Norwegians, Swedes, Danes, and Germans, then with the dialects of Slesvig and of Holstein, the Platt tongue of the Elbe, and the whole jumbled into an inscrutable insular gabble at Heligoland.

English, however, carries you a long way in the North, and broad Scotch helps you further here, and signs do beyond that; and as a last resort you can sketch wants and orders pictorially. It is curious, too, how speedily you acquire foreign words when you are forced to do it; and, moreover, there is a special faculty of the mind, which is marvellously brightened by practice, that of "making people understand," and of "making out what they say."

But this matter of language is made easy by the very fact

of travelling with a canoe, for when a human being comes into a village in this novel fashion, the curiosity to hear from him is so great that the people do all they can to open up communication. If there be one man there who can speak English, French, German, or Latin, be it ever so little and bad, he is sure to come forward, or to be pushed forward, as an interpreter; and, as the newspapers made everybody acquainted with the Rob Roy's progress, there was always some "Dominie Sampson" of the district who came to the front in this way.

Sailors too, it is found, are the most intelligent class to speak with, when you and they have but few words in common. The words they learn of other tongues are just those about the things which you want most to speak of. So the words they know may be few, but they know the useful ones.

As for the more educated class in these southern countries, they are delighted to practise their English or French with a stranger; and often I found school-boys who were learning English so troublesome in their desire to speak with me, that patience was drawn upon largely to satisfy their eagerness.

Instances of this will appear further on, and amusing examples of the struggles they make abroad to pronounce English as we do at home. Therefore, let nobody hesitate to canoe it because he does not know foreign languages; but let no one rely on these to accomplish his tour. In such a voyage, believe me, "gumption" is more useful than German, and friendliness than French.

As for "finding the way," that is entirely another matter; for the natives cannot tell you what they themselves do not know, that is, the route by water even in their own *locale*. In a river it is not often difficult to find the way, though hard enough sometimes to keep in it safely. You have only to hit the right branch, and then to go on down stream, taking a little care not to go to the bottom.

In this northern tour, among lakes and intricate seas, it was not so easy to manage. In these places there is either no current to guide you, or an unseen one that deceives, and there are countless islands to mislead. You sit so low in the boat that one tree-clad rock may hide for an hour the very bay you are in search of. The sun behind the clouds is no index, and the wind changes with every bend of the shores. A compass, unless the needle is six inches long, only puzzles your pate. It gives the general direction; but what you want is the right or left of a particular islet perhaps only a hundred yards long. Still one charm of the canoe trip is this very demand upon that instinct—for, after all, it is something like the faculty of an animal—which, being developed by months of travel in this manner, enables you to say with confidence, "I feel sure that the inlet to the village is behind that rock."

In most of these lakes you cannot *inquire* your way. There is nobody to inquire from. You are going where nobody else goes, and so nobody knows the way to it, and nobody could make you understand it, if he tried. "The map ought to help, then," it may be said. Yes, the map helps much in the easy places, but it confuses you in the hard ones.

Say you get among the 1400 islands in the Malar Lake; why, there are not thirty of them marked even on the largest map. But you cannot tell which of the wooded points and hills around are the marked islands. You do not see all round, or half round any of them, and the end of a large island may appear from your boat like the body of a small one, or a little one near you will obscure two big ones further off.

The island of Onson in Venern, which looks clear enough on the map (at page 48), was so like many others not marked on the map, when seen in actual existence from the water, that it cost me three or four landings and climbings before I could make sure on the subject.

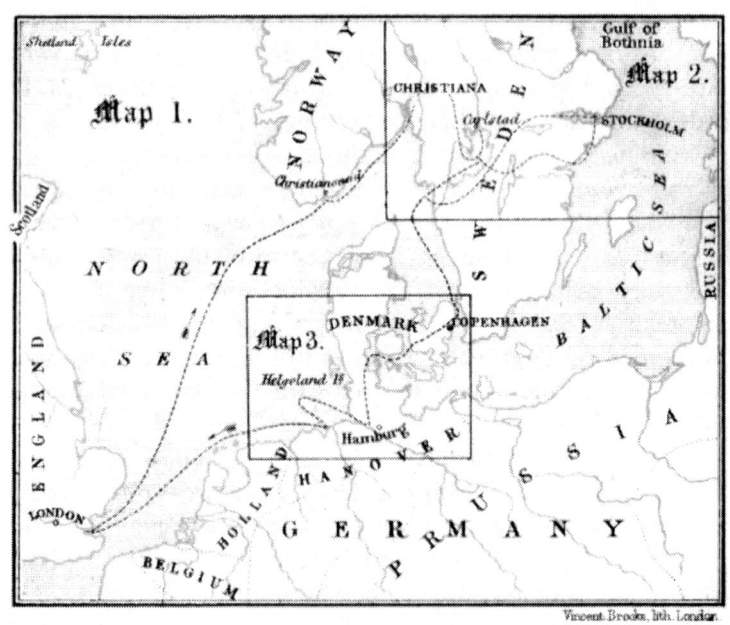

Vincent Brooks, lith. London

## SKELETON MAP I.

*on small Scale shewing the route of the Canoe by a dotted line. Of this the part marked Map 2. will be found separate and on a larger Scale, also the part marked Map 3 at the page stated in the "Illustrations".*

From all this it will be gathered that if there are, say, twenty islands in the way, it is fallacious to measure the distance between any two villages by scale on a map, as if you have only to paddle that number of miles; and yet that it is happy for you—as it was with me almost every day—to have the time, energy, weather, and inclination to make a zig-zag progress such as that marked on Map 4, and thus to see many hidden beauties, while the distance traversed is double that of the direct course. So much for the general subject; meantime we are not troubled with difficulties of this sort, for we are only as yet in a well-linked chain of water.

But this chain very soon gets entangled and knotty, for logs of timber float around us as we near a saw-mill, and at length they block the channel completely across. After once or twice dragging the boat round, and taking my luggage in a second trip, we came one evening to a timber block extending fully a mile. No one was in sight, and I was nonplussed, but as things always turn up if you have patience, I established my cookery under the arch of a bridge, and while at supper a boy came. We gave him some coffee, and when he was in good humour we offered him a sixpence if he would get two men, and this he faithfully did.

Fiery sun glittered above next day, and drove me under the shady trees for miles and miles, at the very time when (as I hear now) it was rain and cold in Scotland, and in Switzerland sloppy and miserable. In both my canoe tours the weather has been favourable. Only two wet days last year, and in this summer not one day on which it was too cold to sit in a single coat, not one in which the rain was bad enough to keep the Rob Roy in doors.

But the obstruction of timber logs was a novelty which we had never met in the twelve great rivers of the former voyage.

These logs are cut in the forests, and then tumbled into the water, to find their way down stream. Men with long poles push them into the current when they get embayed in crooked corners. But in August these men are not allowed by the river for this purpose, because the crops are grown up; and so one or two of the logs will get fixed, and then hundreds gradually arriving, and thousands more, the whole water is covered with a brown-coloured raft.

As the rivers are not navigated, this wooden surface is left for weeks untouched; but it is a serious matter for a canoe to come to such a floating barrier. For the logs are too close to each other for any passage, and they are too small and round to allow the canoeist to drag his boat over. Nothing could be done then but to drag the canoe on the grass, and, in order to see how long my traverse might be, I had generally to mount some hill for a view.

Once, in a very lonely spot on the Vrangs, we found the timber reached as far as the eye could see, so we concealed the boat under a dark tree, and then toiled up a hill on a calm, hot day. The view was at once charming and

alarming. Wood, wood, wood, on to the horizon; the wood on shore being green and growing, and every wind of the river entirely covered with dead logs, thousands and thousands, silent and brown. Nobody in sight, and no house; I sat and waited for events, but nothing would happen, nothing seemed disposed to turn up—only birds chirped.

Lunch and a cigar braced me up to the inevitable task, for we must now drag the Rob Roy through the forest, or we must die and be buried there, like the babes in the wood.

This was a heavy piece of work to contemplate, especially as there was no knowing how many miles must be traversed on shore before open water could be found. But I thought of M'Clintock hauling his boats on snow when ice packs blocked up the sea channel, and then I took out all the luggage, and the mast, sails, paddle, floor-boards, etc., etc., and set off with the bundle as a sort of pilot load, so as to find the best route for dragging the boat afterwards, through the dense trees, rough roots, and boggy swamps.

I was lazy at first, owing to the heat, but soon a vigorous spirit got aroused, and the magnitude of the undertaking, its novelty, and the curious plans we had to adopt for getting over dykes, hedges, brooks, and hillocks, not to say the exertion required for penetrating thickets and copses where no man (let alone a boat) had ever roamed, soon became deeply interesting, and we worked for hours at it, until by double journeys both boat and things were all transported to open country once more, and we launched the Rob Roy on its proper element again, with a glorious evening still before us. A deal canoe would have yielded up its slender life in a brief half mile of work like this.

The final block of the kind, near the village of Rastad compelled me to find two men to carry the canoe over the fields to a house, or night would have caught me there. The people seeing her arrive, were more than ever amazed; and, as they knew the river was full of wood for miles, they asked the man in her how he could possibly have come by the Vrangs, and then he shook his head in a grave and mystical way.

Next day the boat was put on a long cart, consisting of one pole and four wheels, and we made two men sit on these and hold the Rob Roy on their knees, so that the bumps and thumps of a road full of ruts were softened for the canoe by two excellent human cushions. This plan answered admirably, and was very comfortable, at any rate for the boat.

"No more wood," they said; the river was henceforth open, so now came the luxury of the voyage. Deep, rapid, winding streams, with fine rocks, very thick trees, leaping trout, great bounding falls, and then for miles along sunny meads, where I cast my red-hackle fly just on the fishes' noses, and wisely reclined with my feet on deck, while they laboriously jumped into the air all on a fine summer's evening.

Query, as a piece of pure casuistry, Is it quite honest to deceive—a man?—No! But a robber?—Doubtful. Well, then, a fish? The feathers at the end of your casting line are—you cannot deny it—a gross piece of humbug.

The wind rose, and we sailed merrily past large flat barges full of crude iron. They struggle up the Vrangs[1] a mile or two, but we must now be near its end. And see how the rocks trend away right and left as we dash out into the deep, dark, lonely Hugen Sje, a lake only four or five miles long, but with waves of its own that will shake my bottles a bit in their basket from Covent Garden.

I had passed into Sweden, for the boundary was near Morast, where the forest is cleft over hill and down dale and along the weary flat, with a broad belt of cleared timber, and with cairns of stones at intervals. This frontier line (just like those in Canada) runs north and south for a thousand miles.

Perhaps it was this long ruled mark on the world that suggested to a philosophical dreamer that we of Earth might endeavour to speak to the people in the moon by planting on the snows of Siberia a triangle of trees, and the *pons asinorum* of Euclid done in fir forests, so that any schoolboy in our pale satellite could see plainly that we worldlings are at least geometers.

In the little inn we found what was plainly a Briton, with dinner done and a large bottle empty. "You are English," said he. "Try some of this ale; it's really good. I'm a citizen of the world; the earth's my home; my carpet bag's my fortune. They don't know I'm here. Ah! ha! try to shut me up, indeed—catch me, first. I proposed the telegraph line to Capital speculation, too. They sentenced me to prison in France. You're to sleep here. It's a double-bedded room, no doubt, but I don't like that. Well, you may have one bed, as you're English. Don't be alarmed, for I speak in my sleep and walk about the room in the dark."

"Not at all frightened," said I; "and mind you don't grope near me in the dark, for I've an unfortunate habit of hitting right and left—arms rather strong—been paddling for a week." Then he chuckled, and said, softly, he would tell me of a really wonderful phenomenon he had found in the room: "The washing things, &c., are made of clear glass." And so they were!

Out of his carpet bag rolled sovereigns, shirts, shoes, and guide books, all in a muddle; but I gobbled up an omelette, and my sleep was sound after a hard day's work.

### END NOTES

1—Was the Verangian guard of Northmen at Constantinople 700 years ago from this river, and did their word *kyak* for a boat become *caique* in Turkey?

# CHAPTER IV.

Bivouac — Stick to the Boat — Thirty Miles a Day —
Politeness — Dame Cyclops — Miss Kjerstin — Dazzled —
Elga Lake — Pike and Cream — Sluggard — A Little Bill.

DURING the last few days we had most of the incidents
that were met in the former tour—shallows to wade in, falls
and weirs to lower the canoe over, trees to stoop under,
rapids to dash through, and then the novel times with the
logs of timber.

But from henceforward a change occurred, and quite
new features marked the voyage. No more wading or weirs
or logs, and but few rapids and falls, for we had entered a
chain of lakes more or less beautiful, and of all varieties in
size, shape, and depth, in colour and kind. To view these
from the top of a hill was at first delightful, but on reflecting
how far I had to work through that maze of water dotted
over miles of wooded country, and every inch to be gained
by the paddle blades (for the course was still east and
against the wind), the question arose, "How will the biceps
of my arm feel by the time we reach that distant thing over
there—the lake which, like a patch of silver, glitters from far
in the sunbeam?"

New experience, too, had to be learned in the bivouac
line. For it is easier to find a good cooking- place in a river
than at one end or other of a lake; and it would never do to
go edging along the shores to look for a dining-room,

though my usual course was each day to go serpentine till I tired, and then straight to the roosting-place for the night.

On the other hand, when we get hungry in the river, it is enough to begin to "look out," say at 11 a.m., and a good spot is always found before noon—either a tree, or a hay-shed, or a waterfall, or a secluded bank—the best, of course, being some kind of hut, where water will be soonest boiled for soup or chocolate, as the lamp is protected from the wind.

But in choosing a cooking-place on a wide lake or the sea-shore, there are several requisites to be borne in mind as you paddle along, and with keen, empty hunger quickening your choice.

The place, then, must be shaded from sun, sheltered from wind, without flies, but with plenty of dry wood for a glorious bonfire, near good moorings and calm water, perfectly sequestered, and therefore an island is best, where your cork life-preserver makes a good dry seat, and there are suitable stones for a table and kitchen, a soft bank to lie upon, and a pretty view to look upon all the time.

Two hours will be spent here in fixing up, cooking, and cooling down the viands, eating them, and a sweet siesta; so it is worth while to search for a really good place, and when you leave it there is even an affectionate regret at the parting. The nook has been your kitchen, dining-room, and study, and many a look is cast back on it as the smoke still curls up from the logs; nay, the big trees you set a-blazing at first are not yet done smouldering as you shove off to leave them.

Experience had also to be wrought out in the matter of weather, for last year's fair day's voyage did not teach me what to do in rain. Therefore, now in a storm of it, sometimes we drew into shore, and went under a tree for shelter—the larch tree was found to be far the best for resisting a long and heavy down-pour. On two occasions we tried to elude the worst by leaving the boat, but both were sad failures. In the first we were in a most wild lake (without any name), and the edges were bleak banks of rushes. A black nimbus climbed the sky, and darkness was in its cold breath, which we knew was to be followed by a regular drenching.

The Rob Roy was pressed with eager speed to the inhospitable shore; and after half-an-hour's scramble to get on more solid land, and a vain effort to obtain the least atom of help in a village, there was nothing to be done but to re-embark, thoroughly discomfited, and thoroughly soaked. This was the only occasion when I could not find any help; but recollect they did not see the boat; it was hidden in the rushes, and I ought never to have left her so, and sorely we suffered for the blunder. The other instance, teaching the same lesson, will be related further on.

It will be understood that the main design of this canoe voyage was, in the first place, to go by water from Christiania to Stockholm; and already we had done the part never accomplished before by any boat, and only possible for a canoe. From henceforth deep-water lakes and sea fjords would more often be my road. All of them were interesting in beauty, wildness, colour, or contour, while none were positively grand. Every day was very pleasant, and in most the weather was exactly the thing—cool, sunny, and bright, with plenty of wind. The change from river to lake was like that in riding from a green lane to a wide plain. And sometimes, too, this change was a surprise, for all the lakes are not marked in the map. Between the Vinger Sje and the Hugn Sje there are eight separate lakes, but look on the Map No. 2, at page 48, and you do not see one.

For a week the wind had been south-east, that is, just in my teeth, but the sailing days were to come, on fresh water and salt, and my arms were now well braced up to 30 miles a day,[1] even with the wind ahead, but in the finest temperature imaginable for muscular exertion and appetizing toil.

As I rejoiced in this success, and kept pondering in

silence to find out any imaginable improvement to be suggested in the canoe, I began all at once to feel there was a sensible current in the lake, now narrowed to a river-like creek, and at last actually going under a bridge, and thus into the long and lovely lake beyond.

Rocks covered with spruce, larch, and beech, and of every shape and curve, with bays, promontories, and islands, opened in gradual panorama as we passed along; and a gladsome buoyancy of spirit in the fine fresh breeze forced me to shout and sing aloud and alone, or to whistle in bright merriment gaily by the hour. Life of any other sort seemed tedious compared with this, and travelling in any other way a bore.

The houses dotted here and there are red in colour, all of wood, large, and well lighted. Most of the men wear caps, as the Russians do; and there are real flowers sometimes in the women's hair—a pretty fashion. They all salute the passer by, and even some women, who curtsey politely. This is all very nice to see, to praise, and to wish for; but it would be irksome for a profoundly practical people, such as we are, to waste so much time on this particular duty, though certainly we often omit these proper amenities where they ought to be attended to. Swedish politeness, if observed in Piccadilly, would require every man who has friends to carry a hat in his hand. For the sake of his head, indeed, and of neuralgia, he might also have another hat in its usual place.

The change from the Norwegian to the Swedish language was pretty clearly marked, and though we had been twice before in Sweden, it was necessary now to acquire the "Svenske" tongue anew, that is, of course, the few needful words which six days will easily give to anyone who keeps his ears open and his wits about him.

The Ranke See was my next lake, a long and pretty course; but we must shorten the narration of these delightful days, for repetitions, even if pleasant in fact, are

tedious in telling, and still worse to read. Indeed, the time
and muscle consumed in the actualities of this northern tour
are so great a draught upon energy, that we may be excused
from any attempt at making a handbook for canoeists here,
and we must be content to notice the salient features of
some typical events. The weather still continued
magnificent, with only a few heavy showers, and in a fine
sunny evening we landed at the end of the lake Eanke, and
walked up to a house where was a very old woman with
one eye. She was terribly puzzled when I invaded her
cottage on the cliff, and urged her to come and see the boat.
But when she had seen the skiff she at once took a motherly
interest in the skipper, and we carried the Rob to a
cowhouse, where it was hid in the rafters, while I took my
luggage to a very fine farm-house, and knocked, and
walked in.

Mr. Svenson received me rather coldly at first, but soon
he, too, became interested; and I find it best not to ask
immediately for night quarters, rather to leave to the host at

the proper time to give himself the pleasure of offering these. This, then, he kindly did, and going upstairs we found his wife reading a great Bible, and both of them were delighted to examine my little canoe Testament, one which has been a good deal battered about by use in the open air.

The three comely daughters of the mansion vied with each other in attention, and all of us went down to inspect the canoe.

Hitherto they had been coldly hospitable, but now a complete change immediately followed. "They came, they saw, I conquered." Luggage may be brought by a tramp, but a boat—and such a boat!—could not but certify the traveller, and arouse due enthusiasm. Triumphant progress, therefore, of the canoe on the shoulders of Thorsten and Oswald, ploughboys, proud to bear her home—grand concert in her honour—admission free. So while Miss Kjerstin played the guitar and sang the spirited songs of Sweden, I sketched the view of the lake from the window, and a likeness of the girl herself, which being done with a few complimentary touches pleased her and all the servants immensely, and the portrait was duly ensconced on the wall. Here, indeed, was a group for a painter; the father demure and satisfied, the mother staid and watchful, and the bright young girl tinkling the wires of the guitar with a simple innocent look, but withal a proud one, not dismayed.

A maiden at music always seems to me the most nervous of trials. Speaking in public, for a man, is nothing to it. He can stare at the starers, but a girl has to sing under the close scrutiny of others which she may only know with averted eyes. I wonder how they ever can do it in company without making every note a *tr*.

Then we had bacon, and pancakes, and potatoes, and rice, and milk, the farmer and his guest apart from others, and the wife waiting on both; and I gave madame half a pound of the best rice from London, for which she curtsied deeply, and shook hands. The son came in from the fields, a fine young fellow, rather Italian in face, and singing comic songs and warlike marches until I went to my bed-room.[2] The hostess remained a long time with me there examining our canoe kit, and at length I resolved to return to the sitting-room below, and to give them all a treat with the magnesium wire. So we burned a piece amid the crowd of hinds and damsels, whereat arose a shriek of wonder, and before it had subsided, or they could see anything at all, after gazing on the blinding light, their necromancing guest had escaped to bed.

Farmer Svenson had sent me up to bed in comfort, and his assiduous hospitality began early next day with the glass of schnaps, which seems to precede every meal, and to follow it also, intervening, besides, on all sorts of pretexts at other times; for instance, if you eat a mouthful of salmon, it is a positive rule that you must drink a glass of "brandivin," and if a friend meets you, another glass must be taken to greet him.

The Rob Roy was put on a cart, and amid bows and smiles (and perhaps one sigh from Miss K— ) the farmer started his horse for Sulveeka, and acted as driver himself, partly as a compliment to me, and partly to have a thorough good gossip with everybody we met by the way, and a sort of general lecture to the villagers on the beach of the beautiful Elga Lake, on which we now launched the little canoe. The waves from a head-wind dashed so often over the deck that I resolved at last to land at a great saw-mill, observed not far off, and get a cork to bung the mast-hole, also some bread to stop the manifest gap in the captain's own personal hull. At once a crowd of workmen rushed around the new visitor, and I was startled by a voice, "Goot maw — ning, Capiteen." This man had seen the boat some days before, and as I had told the officer of the Landvehr I was also a little in the same line as himself, the title and rank of the paddling Briton were already known at Elga. We sent a lad for two pennyworth of bread, but, meantime, the master of the works sent a pressing invitation to breakfast at his house, while his son, a gentlemanly youth, came to urge the request, and the big dog Hector said the same. There was a doubt as to yielding, till a young lady, a sister, smiling and fair, added her entreaty, and that, of course, settled the matter. Then we were escorted to a fine large wooden chateau, where Mr. Rhodin soon established the hungry paddler beside a dainty meal of pike and strawberries and cream. (N.B. Third breakfast, already, to-day.) All the family and the "gouvernante," she speaking English- perfectly, had a chat about my tour, my boat, and my ideas of Sweden; and when at last the time came for a start, the numerous workmen lined the wharf as we dashed out, thoroughly prepared to face a strong "sou'-easter," from which, indeed, there was no escape.

Among the other arrangements of the boat, I have a cork seat, nine inches square, which can be speedily bound round my waist as a life-buoy when a precaution of this kind may be necessary, but it had not yet been used in actual earnest. The native newspapers in one instance spoke of the canoe as "being carried round my waist," and no doubt it is to this waist-belt of cork that they referred, with a somewhat confused idea of the whole affair. An hour's hard pull on this rough water (with the pike and cream and strawberries), caused me to land and to sound the pumps, and the canoe had more water in than ever before or after. There were thirteen spongefuls, for it is by this I measured the water in the hold. After rounding a point I perceived a boat tossing about with rather a helpless air, and was surprised to find a woman rowing in it all alone; so we went rapidly to assist her. But she was emulous of my speed, and could not so easily be caught, and by no means sought either help or sympathy; nay, she excused herself for being beaten in the race because her boat was so large. Suddenly the wind dropped, and the water calmed as soon, so rapid are the changes from squalls to calms on these lakes; and so

I fished, sailing now with a leading wind to the pleasant, busy town of Arvika, where we rested the Sunday.

A few hours' residence in a small place like this identifies a traveller, if he has arrived in an odd way, as I did. By eleven o'clock every boy and girl in Arvika3 knew the face of the Englishman who came sailing in a *kyak,* and now walked about in a straw hat, genially smiling. The town was pretty to look at, and dull to live in, and a number of tipsy men wandered about in the evening after church Let us have a quiet walk through the wood, sweetly odorous of pine gum, and musical with insect hums. See there the busy ants tracking a broad path over grass and ferns, bustling and jostling and struggling with tiny muscles, to bring home every one his load. Well might the wise man bid us all go to the ant to learn. The lesson is not only for the sluggard, or rather we are all sluggards compared with what we might be, and ought to be; but did you ever see an idle ant? This community of pigmies have a sort of Fleet Street of business in their ant-walks. The rustling of the leaves under their busy feet is quite audible in the silence around. Each little atom (as it seems to be) has yet a mind and a will and a plan, in its own small way. Every ant seems to run everywhere, and to try everything, until he finds some burden to take up, and then an hour is not too long to carry it right to the end. If he cannot find work below, he climbs up a tree. He tumbles three feet to the ground, rolls over, gets up and shakes himself, not a whit the worse, but at it again with vigour. Fancy an Alderman falling from the cross of St. Paul's in his way to the City, and then after all arriving in good time at his office!

In this ant-world there is a crowd, but not confusion. There is activity, but not hurry. They are all intent on a future, and provident of the present. They help one another, and their path is homeward, with room for all to walk in it, yet it lies in a sure direction. A few minutes spent by an ants' nest is generally a good lesson of life, yes, and of morals. "Learn of her ways, and be wise."

Night has come now, and as the moon sails out on the lake there is soft music under the window, and gentle voices of girls singing very pretty Swedish hymns; and then all is soothed into the quiet of dark repose, except the prosy old watch man, who intones the hour through his nose, or blows so many bass notes, sounding the clock on his horn.

Here is the hotel bill, merely as a specimen :

No. 6.

| 1866. | | | | | | | | |
|---|---|---|---|---|---|---|---|---|
| 11/8. | Afton, ½ öl | . | . | . | . | Rd. | ·91 | öre. |
| 12. | Kaffe | . | . | . | . | . | ·50 | „ |
| | Middags, ½ öl | . | . | . | . | . | 1·16 | „ |
| | Tobak | . | . | . | . | . | ·50 | „ |
| | Afton | . | . | . | . | . | ·50 | „ |
| 13. | Caffe | . | . | . | . | . | | |
| | Logi | . | . | . | . | . | 2·50 | „ |
| | Frukost | . | . | . | . | . | ·50 | „ |
| | | | | | | Rd. | 6·57 | |

Quiteros Arvika, 13 Aug., 1866.                    T. F. W.

A rix-dollar is worth about 14d. English, and contains 100 öre, so the whole amount is under 8s.

## END NOTES

1—Equal to 40 miles in known water.

2—One of these national airs will be found further on (page 143). A famous Swedish singer, spoken of with rapture as equal to "Jenny Lind," is Christina Neillson. Every third woman here is Kerstin, and every fourth man is Neillson.

3—This is the Oscarstadt of Hagelstan's map.

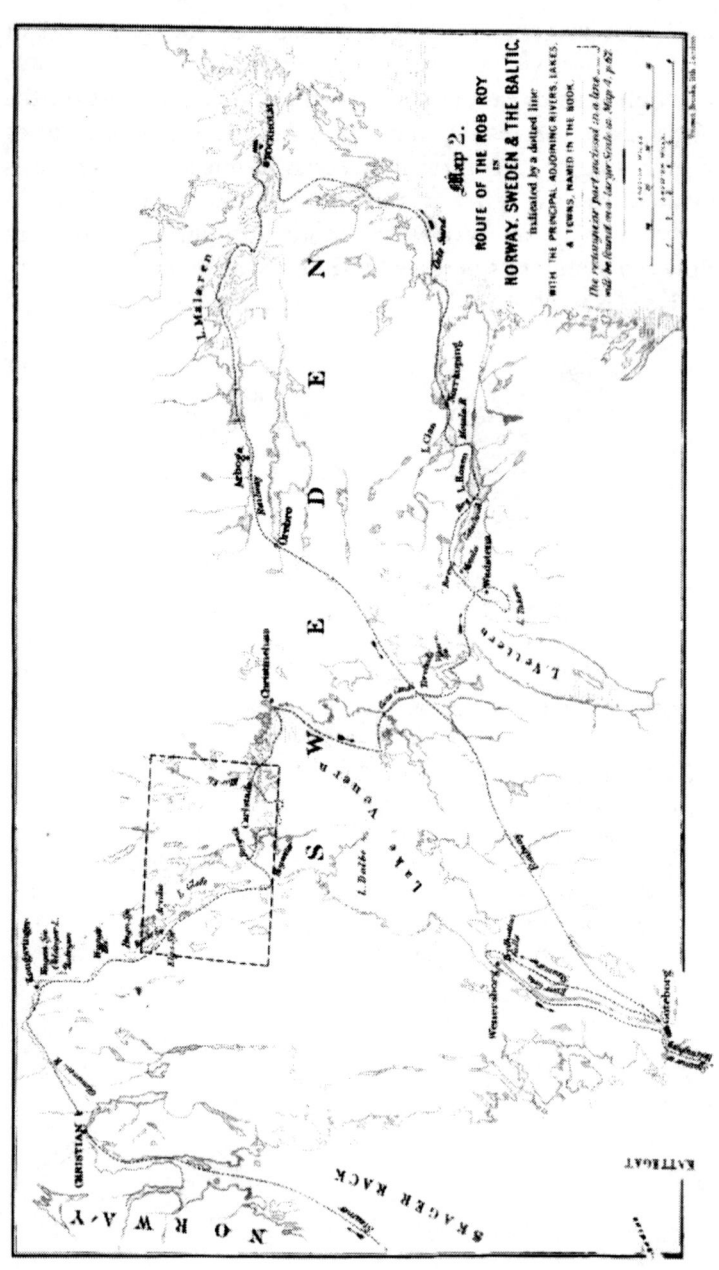

Map 2.

ROUTE OF THE ROB ROY
IN
NORWAY, SWEDEN & THE BALTIC.

Indicated by a dotted line:

WITH THE PRINCIPAL ADJOINING RIVERS, LAKES
& TOWNS, NAMED IN THE BOOK.

*The rectangular part enclosed in a line
will be found on a larger Scale at Map 4. p 227*

# CHAPTER V.

A Hundred Luncheons — Luxury — Wake Up — Wait for
Events— John Bull at Home — Vermland — Model Wife —
Chat in Latin — Manners.

IT was a lovely morning when we left Arvika, and with
all energy renewed after the Sunday's rest. A gauzy haze
around the dawn melted away into a clear blue sky, and the
lovely Elga Lake was rippleless. No sounds came from the
shores, no singing from the woods, and as I quietly
skimmed along even the ticking of my watch was easily
heard; for the hollow cedar boat probably acted like the
body of a piano or a guitar.

The light-houses on the lakes and inland lagoons are
sometimes very small. A mere glass box upon a stand, of
which you can touch the top, is placed on a jutting rock; and
the village lamplighter comes to put it to rights in the
evening, while during the day the crew of the Rob Roy land
and stretch their legs beside the tower.

Here there were most inviting islands for he bivouac.
We could have lunched a hundred times, and never within
sight of the same place twice. But in the sole dinner I did
take, a phenomenon appeared which was not at all
picturesque; for, in preparing my cookery, the spirit-lamp
exploded, and nearly burned some of the crew, but we soon
made a good fire of wood, and it went on bravely burning,
long after "the gentlemen had left the dining-room."

PHAROS MINOR.

"Steward!" "Yes, Sir." "You may take away the things."
The spoon is long and narrow, so that you can eat an egg
with it, and for stirring up the coffee or soup or chocolate
this weapon is useful enough; but practically the fork was
never in requisition, and that end of the implement may be
regarded as a fond conceit.

As the scenery was so fine, and the pleasant day was all
before us, and no halting place had been settled for the
night, we devoted an hour or two to make some
experiments as to the speed of the boat, and other like
matters which a perfect calm is favourable for ascertaining.

It appeared, then, that in paddling well but steadily
there were 100 double strokes (that is, one on each side)
made in five minutes; which, at the speed of six miles an
hour, would give 200 double strokes in a mile. Counting
stoppages, rests, and hindrances, it will be found that three
miles an hour is enough in continuous touring, and in still
water, in fact, a good walking pace; but then of course on a
river you gain at the rate of two or three miles more by
current for long stretches.

On the whole we may say three miles an hour on lakes
and four on rivers for easy paddling. The zigzag course of

the Rob Roy here is marked in Map 2, where you see that the shores of the lake gradually approach until we enter the Glava Fjole, its waters curling under a delicious breeze from the northwest, and so enabling me for the first time in this voyage to set sail—a most grateful pleasure.

As the rocks grew higher and nearer, and the sun more hot, so the breeze also increased, until we scudded away at a famous pace, while I stretched at full length, with my head leaning back on the adjustable backboard (the comfort of one's life in a canoe), and my feet spread out on deck, and bright clear waves lapping my hands now and then, or daringly kissing my cheek.

The luxury of this rest (without stopping) after the hard tugs against the east wind last week, will always be remembered by the passengers of the canoe.

To vary the amusement, I bent my course here and there, into this bay on the right, and round that cape on the left; now chasing a duck that kept diving and diving before me, and again running close to some little village, where all the folks came out, but saw a boat pass through them without its once allowing any face to be seen. *Their* account of the phantom craft that passed them I should very much like to hear.

The work of a long summer's day, even with its rests and detours and many stoppages, had brought me thirty miles on my route, and as the sun drooped, so died away the wind; but the water closing now to the breadth of a river, with a steady current, still carried us on through the Bjorno Sje, the Lake of the Bears.

Over the waving weeds, fast by the dipping bushes, great rocks above us, and health and peace within, it was all in a mellow light of gloaming, such as that picture shows us, "With the Stream."

I fished the while—as comfortable in my boat as you are on your sofa—use makes it so. At last I was lazy, and so were the fish, for they jumped only half way to the fly, and seemed to lollop about for play, and did not "mean business." We were all so pleasant and comfortable—the canoe, the fisherman, and the fish—that by consent it was agreed to "make believe," on all sides, until, I do believe, our coxswain nodded in the sultry air, and then he fell fast asleep.

At this time the Rob Roy was borne on the smooth current, stern-foremost, side-foremost, any way; all discipline was unloosed, and no one was on the watch, as we drifted in among the long stakes, which were leaning down as they bent to the stream, and murmuring at the pressure with an audible thrill.

Suddenly I was aroused by a tremendous tug at my fishing-line. In an instant it was "all hands on deck," and a rattling of paddles and spars and a clattering of shoes. What a huge salmon it must be we are catching. It has pulled the whole boat round! Haul away cheerily.

Ah! my hook had caught a tree!

Again the lake narrowed between fine cliffs into a flowing neck of bright clear water, and the river stream bore the canoe gently on until evening, when the mirthful lass at the ferry told me I could sleep at a house on the knoll above.

No person is in sight as we draw to shore, and in the earlier days I should have been anxious about how to manage alone. But experience proves that a few minutes always brings some one within hail, in such places, if any one house is visible; and the infinite variety of ways in which apparent difficulties solve themselves by a little patience, and keeping "your weather eye open," really constitute one of the amusing characteristics of the voyage.

Lazy after long sailing (which stiffens one considerably, and indisposes for more exertion), we waited as the sun went down, and the cool silent stream flowed by, and nobody came, and nothing happened. There seemed to be a spell over all of listless inaction. Then I beckoned to the pretty ferry girl, and she rowed over, laughing. "I am an

Englishman," said I. She told me "Osterman could speak English." "Osterman—Osterman!" I repeated; " what can be the meaning of Osterman?" And then to her, "Tell me plainly, miss, what is Osterman? Is it a man fishing for oysters?" She answered, "Osterman is just Osterman;" and very soon he came on the scene himself—a fine young fellow; his name was Osterman, he spoke English well, and had 400 hooks with him, and a lad to set the night-lines. He objected at first to delay his fishing, or to let the boy carry my boat; but persuasion prevailed. If it had not done so it would have been a surprise to me, and the first time of failure in securing help by good temper and kind words.

We carried the canoe to a private house, and she was soon locked up, and the key of the barn in my pocket. This mode of establishing the Rob Roy in night quarters has merits and disadvantages; although it is secure it is troublesome, for over and over the key has to be produced for new comers, who enter humbly, cap in hand, to ask for a sight of the "leety bote." When I was dining a man came up-stairs, and in the shyest manner entered into conversation, each of us talking quite independently of the other, but probably edified, without any distinct allusion to each other's arguments. He turned out to be the proprietor of the house. How modest, how courteous, how gentle was this plain cottier, and how few people (I could not help thinking) would have been so delicately attentive if, on coming home at night, they found a stranger comfortably eating their best fare!

Desperate sticklers we may be for Old England and everything English; but repeated lessons abroad have at length forced me to confess that, in comparison with most of these "outlandish folks," we English are often very boorish; and the conviction of this may well make us behave in foreign lands with the modesty of those who feel their countrymen have much to learn.

The fire-place here was on a triangular hearth, about the

height of a chair, and in the middle of the room. It was arched over so as to form a chimney, and a sketch of it will be found on page 112, (fig. 1). This excellent arrangement is one of the best to be seen for comfort and convenience, because, while the fire is in fact open, it has still a snug chimney corner, and you can cook on it or sit by it without having to stoop far. The man, so demure and attentive, wore a leather apron, and at first we thought he was a blacksmith, but it was soon seen that all the working men wear these aprons to protect their knees and bodies from the wear and tear of implements, as well as from rain.[1] The worthy host accepted a tract, and at once began reading it aloud, and half an hour afterwards we could hear him still going on, while his head was nodded, or thoughtfully shaken, as he seemed to feel the sense of the Swedish message from England. All this was in the district of Vermland, a region little seen by travellers, and seen, perhaps, by no one as the captain of the canoe saw it. Still you may see a bit of it on the Map opposite. But the fame of it is of quaintness, respectability, prejudice, patriotism, and open hospitality. Unawares, we had paddled into the Highlands of Sweden.

Next day we had to charter a little waggon to carry the Rob Roy from this chain of waters to the end of an arm of the great Venern See, a splendid lake about 100 miles long, only less than the lakes Ladoga and Onega of European waters. We soon slung the canoe upon two ropes; one of them was made of pig's hair, which is said to last a long time even when used in rain and frost The *portage* was seven or eight miles, and gave me a pleasant walk alongside the cart, the man wondering (and mumbling his wonder all the time) that the Herr would insist upon walking along a road plashy and wet; but stately trees and graceful ferns adorned it, and painter's glimpses through the forest and over the lakes. Then came we to Borgivik—full of smoke and din, with tilt-hammers worked by gushing waterwheels, and grimy Titans swaying brawny arms among the sparks and fire-flakes, as the ground quivered at each blow on the molten mass.

I drove the cart through a wondering crowd right up to the house of the proprietor of the works, Mr. Almquist, who received us with great courtesy, while his excellent wife appeared in the kitchen ruling the pastry and etceteras which are so numerous in Swedish cooking.

I thought at first she was the cook, but when I gave her my wet things to be dried in a very matter-of-fact way (as one must push a little), she took them with so much readier politeness than the servant by her side, that I scarcely wondered afterwards to find her in the drawing-room playing Weber's *Preciosa* with a tasteful touch of the finger-board not at all spoiled by an hour or two at the "dresser." This is the sort of wife that it is happy for a traveller to visit. The lady and her husband may possibly read these lines—as many Swedes have promised to do—and let it be understood that the thanks of a wandering Englishman are here conveyed to the courteous and hospitable Vermlanders.

Rolf and Bruno, the dogs, soon made friends with me; but none of the family could speak English or French, so my stock of Swedish being soon exhausted, we had to depend on mutual smiles; until the amiable host pointed to a line in a phrase book, which said, "You are very welcome;" and I answered by another, "I am exceedingly comfortable, and much obliged."

However, Dr. Somebody came to tea, and we talked Latin with that circumlocutory elegance which a very slow remembrance of it involves, like pumping water out of a very deep well, with very little in the bucket when it comes up, and not much at the bottom.

I had broken my watch-glass, and they had not one small enough in the village shop, but we procured a large one, fitting about as well as a saucer; and, after some experiments, I discovered that, by putting a piece of gauze[2] over this great glass, the watch-dial could be seen perfectly, and yet the hands were protected. This may be considered a useful invention—at any rate it was so for me, until next day a man said—a stranger, too, "Give me your watch, and I will return it with a glass to-morrow at half-past five." We could not but trust the honest Swede, and faithfully the watch arrived, with an excellent patent glass upon it, which has been thumped and bumped ever since, and, indeed, is even cracked, but is still serviceable.[3]

Everything in this house was substantial, airy, clean, punctual, and good. The boys were well behaved. The visitors listened with smiles to our mangled Latin, the lady beamed with benevolent motherly kindness, and all for a strange traveller, who had no possible claim upon their time and attention but that he was a stranger—and had a canoe. In Norway and Sweden all who are seated at dinner rise at the end, and bow to the host, and thank him for his hospitality. As for breakfast it is taken as a peripatetic meal—the viands being attacked from front and rear and flanks, as you cut in and snap a bit, and then trudge about the room. It is an uncomfortable fashion, and more especially so in an inn, where a dozen heavy-heeled men, with hoarse voices and champing jaws, stump round and round on the wooden floor, all talking, eating, and smoking in independent circles about the table.

Tea is sometimes taken at night; and what do you think of the accompaniment of a plate of thick pea-soup instead of muffins?

## END NOTES

1—Some of the schoolboys have leather kneecaps, and we noticed one little fellow with brass ends to his boots, which, no doubt, is a good plan for moderating papa's bill at the shoemaker's.

2—Brought for a mosquito veil, but no mosquito ever came.

3—For boating, the watch ought to be carried on a small pocket near the collar-bone, where it is the least likely to get smashed, and is most likely to be kept dry when you have to jump into the water or to swim.

# CHAPTER VI.

Caught in a Squall — Lost! Lost! Lost! — Cholera Ward —
Alone in a Lantern — A Strange Duet — On Deck — French
Sailors — Yankee — Cockney — Cauliflowers.

EARLY next day the whole family and the mechanics
came with me to the water, and the Rob Roy shoved off into
a squally sea; for it may really be called a sea, this noble
lake of Venern. All hats were off, and warm adieux wished
"happy travel" to the little boat, no doubt the smallest craft
that had ever ventured on this great lake. For an hour or
two the course was among landlocked bays and high hills,
with dense wood to the water's edge, and we did not feel
the strength of the breeze there; but, on facing round the
last lonely wooded point, the white waves, and angry
clouds, and thick drizzling rain, show that full steam must
be put on if we mean to reach Carlstadt to-night, and I must
reach it, for letters are to be there, and my packet of reserve
provisions.

Three grand points I had settled for this tour; to paddle
on Venern, on the Baltic, and on the Great Belt in Denmark.
Here was number one feat approaching fulfilment, but a
more unpromising day could not have opened. Wind, rain,
and fog, seldom you have the three at once; but each of
them now was vigorous in opposing me, and any one of
them alone would have been reason enough to defer the
attempt. Therefore I landed where I could ponder half-an-
hour, with a cigar, and consult with the boatswain and mate

over our chart; and the question was solemnly debated, "Is it not foolish to go on with thirty miles before me in this whistling mist, and on this huge lake?"

A black squall then varied the dull grey of the horizon, and I had to land for shelter while its fury was spent on the rocks above me. Bright sun followed, and then came another portentous cloud, so I resolved to dine at the very next house to be met; but it was a miserable hut, and the poor man in it had no bread. Things looked awkward now, with so much delay and so long a day's work to be done, so we made for another island, hard by the narrow strait of Asunda, where was the last house to be met for many hours. In this poor fisher's hut we found two sailors and a rosy-faced boy, eating fish and potatoes with their hands, and a woman sat by with a very dirty baby, which, she covered with kisses. I produced my little packet of sugar and gave the baby some, and mamma soon got me some bread, and I joined in the wooden bowl of potatoes, and cooked my coffee by their fire, and sketched, and gave her some of the finest rice from Fortnum and Mason's, and let off a wax match, and gave two to a boy, and, in fact, made myself generally agreeable. This was the first instance in which we found a man who could not read; still he managed to decipher the obverse of a coin, and so we departed with thanks to all, but without kissing the child.

Then into the tumbling waves, aha! How cheery the motion is with a dash and a rush, and the sea-bird's scream aloft, and the black rocks white with foam around. What other mode of travel is so pleasant as this? The numerous islands were soon so perplexing that I had to land, first upon Sande Isle, and then on several others, climbing each time some lonely peak to see where I ought to go; for the islands are in the way of your seeing them, just as you "cannot see the forest for the trees."

The thick undergrowth and slippery moss on the islands made it tiring work to climb. The panorama from the top, too, was not cheering; and once when I had settled on the course, and observed the wind to steer by, and then came down, the wind had actually veered eight points in that ten minutes (as was stated to be the case by a sea captain, next day), so I was utterly puzzled, and in fact started quite in a wrong direction, which would have led me forty miles to the east. There was nothing for it but to climb once more, for it was absolutely necessary to find out the island of Onson among the numerous others in the Katt Fjord; and yet the only point that was unmistakable was the headland at the end of Hammaro, which stood out sharp on the far horizon of indigo blue. Suddenly, and to our great joy, a sun ray broke forth and showed a white puff from a steamer's funnel, so we concluded instantly *that* must be the direction of Carlstadt; and so it was.

By careful steering, and after numerous alterations of my intended course, I happened to go right, and the sun at length overcame the dark clouds around him, shining bright through the fog, and showed me land only seven or eight miles away, but dead to windward. This was a hard pull, yet when I reached the lighthouse and climbed up to it nobody was there; so it was of no use to shout.

We therefore started again, and scrambled on somehow to the mouth of one of the branches of the great Klar river, one of the largest in Sweden; and then in a blazing hot sun that made the marshes reek a pestilent air, we stemmed the current slowly for an hour, amid thousands and thousands of timber logs.

Carlstadt was burned down last year, and cholera had broken out among the poor people housed temporarily on the flat shore, so we were urged to avoid the place as exceedingly dangerous. It was, therefore, with no small pleasure that I found a little steamer alongside the quay. For variety's sake let us put the dialogue in the sensation novel style.

"When do you start?" said I.

"At six to-morrow."

"Eastward?"

"Yes."

"Will you take me?"

"Come along, sir!"

So the Rob Roy was on its deck in a trice, and a messenger brought my "reserve prog" and a letter from home—a better feast! Good kind Captain Dahlander came forward with "How do you do? are you wet?" "Yes, very." "Then change instantly—this is no place to get a chill in;" and in a few minutes I had his big greatcoat around me and a stiff glass of grog inside, and felt all the better for my paddle of twelve hours, and forty English miles of watery wandering on Venern. The glass vessel he poured this opportune brandy from was shaped like a dog, with its tail for a handle, and the fiery fluid came from its mouth. Many days afterwards we had another pull at the tail of the captain's dog.[1]

Next day, after visiting several ports I decided to land on the island of Bromo, where a steamer would pass at night, and might take me to the West Gotha Canal. The canoe was put in a shed, and we had a long walk in a wood, and then inspected the large glass-works on this curious island; and just after we came there the woodwork of the old roof, built sixty years ago, caught fire, and a great bustle was the result.

The evening was cold, and it was tedious work to wait seven hours for a steamer; but the man gave me the key of the lighthouse, and I rigged up my kitchen and made coffee there, and then put on two complete suits of clothes to keep me warm, and paced the little harbour quay until the stars came out. A brilliant meteor shot across the sky, and reminded me that in this particular week of each year a meteoric epoch comes with shoals of shooting stars. Mounting into the lantern of the lighthouse, I sat by the camphine lamp both for heat and light, reading and

sketching and thinking through the heat and light, reading and sketching and thinking through the midnight hours, with a lonely feeling and anxious expectancy of a steamer's whistle in each gust of wind. At length footsteps heard below showed there was some other passenger. He soon began to whistle as he paced back and forward, stamping his feet. To console him, and for company's sake, I whistled a second to his tunes; and thus we went on until our whole stock of Italian and native airs was exhausted by singing and whistling in a strange duet, one performer standing on the pier and the other seated aloft in the lantern.

The steamer came, and it was coolly passing us by altogether, but my comrade hailed them long and loud and often, and they came back grumbling, but not sorry to hear there was an English passenger, though they shouted out that all the cabins were quite full. "Never mind," said I, "the deck will do for me." Anything, to be done with the lantern, where I was so tired and cramped. The deck was piled with three tiers of herring barrels—not a very savoury cargo, but I recollect a far worse one when I went from Valentia to the Balearic Isles with 355 live pigs on deck. For, say that each pig squeaks but once in five minutes—a very moderate allowance surely—and that a good squeak lasts sixty seconds at least; then you have the continuous squeaking of twelve pigs together for twenty-four hours—not counting the grunts or the general odour.

It was a curious passage this, from Bromö, as I sat close to the funnel, and all was dark, except when the furnace doors opened, and their warm redness glared on the hot stokers, and on the moving beams and cranks, till the scene was quenched again in darkness; but the rattling still went on. One side[2] of my face was so hot that I had to screen it, and the other side was so cold in the draught that I had to screen that too. You will find, however, that if you are in good health a night spent thus on deck passes, after all, far better than if from illness or anxiety you toss about through wakeful hours, even in the most comfortable bed.

There is a dreamy poetry about the sea at night, with the illumined heaven above, that seems to sway all the stars to and fro among the ropes, though it is only the vessel that is rolling gently.

Then quiet thoughts of home and home things circle in the mind, and the engine keeps on its ceaseless music, saying every moment over and over what seemed to me like "blong-italong-ee-thang."

The steering from the lake into the canal at night in a fog, and through so narrow a channel that only one foot was to spare on either side, surprised and delighted me. But these Swedes and Norwegians are all good sailors. I recollect meeting our Baltic fleet at Copenhagen when it had cruised six months during the Crimean war. The French fleet came in, too, and the middies and sailors soon hired every possible quadruped at all resembling a horse, and we went scampering over the fields for thirty miles with that uproarious enjoyment which sailors have ashore. Good authority then informed me that the French ships were as well built and equipped as ours, and their gunnery not inferior; but that it was in a certain kind of weather where the difference was seen at once between the nations. When snow, sleet, and rain filled the air, and driving fog darkened the murky night, and the sea and sky seemed one black hazy mass, then the French admiral always signalled, "Let the English vessels lead." Buoys, beacons, and lighthouses had all been removed by the enemy; but the Orkney, and Shetland, and North Sea pilots found their way still. The fleet did not lose one ship, though often the three-deckers had only a yard of water under their keels in drizzly fogs, such was the seamanship of the Baltic pilots.

As at this period of the journey the packet of excellent biscuits in my "reserve luggage" became less bulky, for they were more consumed, there was room left for a few little souvenirs of the voyage. Here is a pretty bag we have brought back. It is a slip of white birch bark, soft and smooth, like satin paper, and bent into an oval shape. By a neat handle you can carry it away full of fresh raspberries, sparkling with cold dew, and bursting with luscious sweetness, all for the sum of one halfpenny.

Here is a batch of Swedish newspapers, each of them describing the Rob Roy; but we know all about her already.

Here again is a small volume, in Swedish, called "The Little American"—the first time we have observed the "greatest nation, sir, on the face of the earth, sir," propound that their language is not "English," however true that may be in cases, and however just may be their right to call it "American." For this blue-book is a sort of school primer, intended to teach the Danes how to pronounce the United-Statesian language, and perhaps we English may have a lesson, too.

In one column of each page is the Danish word or phrase; and in another the same English words written with Danish letters; and in the third column these are written again in Danish letters, as they are to be pronounced; but we will put English letters instead, and the first column may be omitted.

| | |
|---|---|
| (1.) George has been punished by his father. | Dschaardsch has bin ponnisch'd bei hihs fadher. |
| (2.) Amely's shoes are not clean. | Amm'lih's schuhs ahr naott klihn. |
| (3.) Oh, joy! huzza! the pleasure. | Oh, dschei! hoosac! dhe plessjur. |
| (4.) Churchyard key. | Tschortschjard kih. |
| (5.) Geography cheese. | Dschioggraefli Tschihs. |
| (6.) Stay a little. | Steh ae littel. |
| (7.) Your nightcab and bootjack. | Juhr neichtkoopp and buhtdschjackk. |
| (8.) Waiter, the tinder-box. | Huehter, dhe tinder-bokks. |

Sweden and America have the largest lucifer-match manufactories in the world; so we may infer from the last phrase on the list that the book is rather ancient; and the word "Amely" in No. 2, and "æ littel" in No. 6, indicate an American editor; while the errors in No. 7 show that he was very careless.

But, after all, this book is not so bad as the wretched phrase-book sold in London when you ask for the best for learning Danish from, and which as usual says all you don't care to say, and ends by an elaborate list of proverbs, such as, "The tailor makes the man," and "The early bird picks up the first worm;" the very last being "All's well that ends well," which this book does not.

Let those, then, who chide the roving paddler because he wantonly strays where he does not know the tongue—and there are some who would not have us unmoor the canoe until its schoolmaster is a universal linguist—let them club their wise heads together, and their learned tongues, and give the voyaging world a phrasebook worthy of the name. The Rob Roy does not want it, but it would be a good thing to do.

Some years ago three of us being in Copenhagen, and all hungry, we sat down in a restaurant to dine, but the bill of fare was utterly incomprehensible; so we agreed to order the dish which had the longest name. This being selected, the waiter was directed to bring one portion for each of us. Time went, but nothing came. Other people ordered, ate, and left the place, and our hunger was keener every moment, until at length the white-aproned "kypare" brought in a great tray with three huge covered dishes, which were duly placed before us—highly expectant of a treat. When the covers were removed, lo! there were three dressed *cauliflowers!*

## END NOTES
1- See post, p. 161, with a portrait of the spirited animal.
2- "Sidehead," Americè — and why not? though we Britons have only foreheads and blockheads.

# CHAPTER VII.

Ladies' Locks — Tailoring — Canoe Chat — Whispers —
Motala Ström — London Scottish R.V. — Charming Family
— Lake Vettern — For England — Monitors — Sister Craft
— The Gunboat — Morning Call.

JUST as half-past two was "belled" on our little steamer,
the dawn appeared, linking the new day to the past
evening, and making one glad to find that the great World
was not too sleepy to keep turning round.

One after another passengers came up from below, each
more frowsy-looking than the other, and all surprised to
find a little canoe added to the occupants of the deck.

The steamer's swell rushed along the canal banks, and
the tall green reeds bent down in low bows, as if to
acknowledge the power of man, while the waves burst with
a splash among the bushes, and chased the little sea-
sparrows from their night haunts, chirping angrily.

The locks were always opened by women, who worked
famously, though it looked odd enough to see young lasses,
with great crinolines, perched high aloft, and turning the
winch handles. I got ashore and helped them, partly for
exercise, and partly for gallantry.

As morning went on the country girls came to sell fresh
raspberries in pretty baskets of birch bark, and butter, and
woodcocks. I never saw a more pleasant set of fellows than
these Swedes, and they all seem so glad to be thanked for
their attentions.

The steamers on the lakes, and rivers, and canals of Sweden are very well managed, and are comfortable, though their dimensions are necessarily limited by the size of the locks they have to pass through on the canals. The stewardess ("Mademoiselle" you must recollect to call her) is eminently civil, and so is her *aide*—"Lina" you may safely call her, for Caroline is as frequently the name as Mary is with us. A neat bill of fare and good things upon it invite you to eat and drink much, with very little to pay.

Sometimes picnic parties avail themselves of the frequent passing to and fro of these convenient tidy little craft, and a dozen ladies and gentlemen come aboard the steamer for a breakfast, which lasts until the boat stops again, some ten miles away, at the next lock.

My macintosh cape having had various rents and grievances in it, the time was opportune to make a new garment from a piece of leather cloth prudently stored in my reserve luggage.

An agreeable fellow-passenger helped this bit of tailoring, and we first made a pattern from a newspaper; and having improved it to the most fashionable shape, the cloth itself was cut out—a more serious matter. The new robe fitted admirably; it was sure to do so, for it was only a square piece with a hole for the neck, and the copyright (of

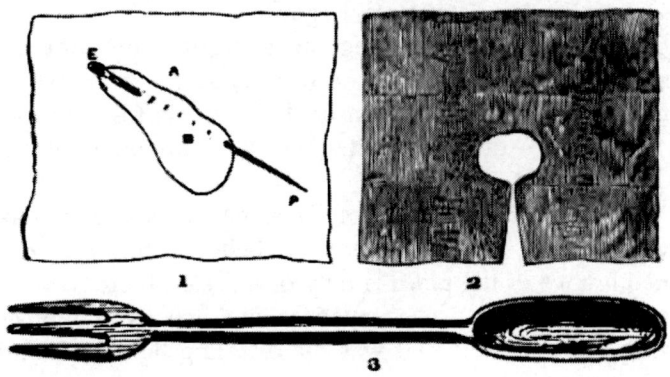

figure 2) is *not* reserved; so any dandy may wear it in Pall Mall.

But this sternly simple garment did excellent service in places where there was nobody to quiz it, and at times when all observers would gladly have shared its shelter.

Meanwhile our crew really must have a snooze, the last forty-eight hours having been rather a strain on our energy, so the starboard watch of the Rob Roy are all piped into their hammocks, while you and the people on deck will have a little chat.

It may be frequently remarked how often foreigners speak loudly to you, when you appear not to understand their tongue in the usual tone. They mistake ignorance for deafness. But at the "Borrullup," the marriage-feast described further on, there was one very communicative man, who always addressed me in a very low whisper, though he spoke loudly enough to other people. The philosophy of this modification to increase the facility of intercourse we could not understand.

Another thing; foreigners conversing together will sometimes sink their voices into almost a whisper, when you may be sure they are talking about "you," and it is impossible then not to overhear their words; whereas, if they kept to the usual degree of voice (which, by the way, is loud and harsh in the North), the whole of the talk would pass unnoticed as a universal jargon.

All the time of this foregoing gossiping interlude you have indulged in about other people, it must be remembered that the captain of the canoe is fast asleep in his hammock—that's why the pen has run on while the paddle was still.

Meantime the West Gotha Canal has led us on to Lake Viken, which is very pretty, I believe; for my own remembrance of the place is only of a dream there, wherein a gigantic paddle was swayed to and fro by a monster having one eye, and that was the dazzling light of Bromö.

But our steamer has now glided along into Lake Vettern, so we are thoroughly awake, and sober sense resumes her throne.

This Vettern lake is quite a sea in size, for though not so broad as the Venern, it is about eighty miles long, as may be seen on Map 2. There are ninety tributary streams to swell its clear waters and only one exit for all the Motala river. Report says that the rise and fall of the water in the lake coincides with that at Geneva, and that both are unaccountable. Crossing the Vettern, we are at pretty Vadstena, where the Mayor called on me (on the Rob Roy, I fancy), saying, "You come here when and where to go?" then again, inquiringly, "On beesness?" "Yes," said I; "on business, to see your very nice town;" so I took a pinch of snuff from his box, and told him that kind was called "Prince's Mixture."

A splendid Aurora lit up the sky at night. Is this not the grandest sight to be seen on earth, with a perfect sense of security all the time?

Next day I hired a vehicle to drive about twelve miles to Kyleberg, where an old friend of mine has fixed his home—a Scotchman born in Sweden. It was rather venturesome to alight at the door without any previous warning; but in Sweden people are as hospitable as the Highland chiefs could be in olden days, and Mr. Axel Dickson received his sudden guest in the warmest manner, speaking with the strong accent of his Scottish ancestry, and grasping my hand with the powerful clutch of his own; and what that is one may conceive when it is mentioned that in our London Scottish corps Mr. Dickson was the "pivot man" of No. 1 Kilt Company, and was, perhaps, the only man in that corps (or any other in London, indeed) who could take up two Enfield rifles by the muzzles and hold them, one in each hand, at full arm's length, with the butts extended.

Kyleberg is pronounced Chilliberch, with the first "ch"

as in "children," and the second guttural "ch" as in the words Loch Lochy, which are unutterable by Cockney lips. Our host's fine mansion here is a specimen of what taste and skill can do when they direct a good long purse.

There is the Scotch steward—Mr. Pennycuik, from Cupar and Angus—talking Swedish like a native, but he "canna mak up his mind jist yet" (fifteen years) as to which of the Svenska damsels ought to share his home. There, too, is the sleek prize bull "Marksman," who bore away the gold medal from all Sweden, and whose babies sell for 5l. each where good calves are in demand.

Such a place—an oasis in the rougher life around—was just the spot to spend my quiet Sunday. Mr. Dickson reads prayers every morning in Swedish; and on Sundays the neighbours do not object to come under his pastoral charge for an hour. But he ministers again there in English, and Mrs. Dickson reads for us in the evening; so that Swedes and Britons all have their share of Sunday.

It was a really pleasant time with this charming family, where refinement and kindness are happily combined; and I left the place not likely to forget my visit to Kyleberg, even after the packet of Scotch oat-cake and the pot of marmalade, thoughtfully given to me at parting, had been finished in the luxury of several bivouacs on less favoured spots.

Returning to Vadstena, we found the interest about the little Rob Roy had permeated the place. There was a meeting of gentlemen to discuss the proposal for lighting their town with gas,[1] and there they asked when the *kyak* was to start, that they might not miss the sight. It was answered that her captain only deferred his start until the end of the meeting, as a friend of his was there. In five minutes, then, the gas matter was settled. All the twenty-four councillors agreed, and the contract was signed, that the canoe might be seen under way.

Meanwhile the boat had been laid out for a thorough

overhaul and examination, this being the first "lawful" day on which she was dry enough to do this. The ship's carpenter duly reported that, with the exception of four ribs broken on the Vinger See, she was perfectly stanch and sound; and so we launched her with confidence on Lake Vettern, under a parting cheer from the assembly on the pier—a cheer being a novelty in the programme, which was no doubt raised from British lungs. The water here was cold and clear and deep, and the bright waves played round the little boat, under a soft warm breeze, enlivening enough, though not in a favourable direction, until we had reached a point where I entered the Motala River, and landed for a few minutes' rest, and to set sail and run before the wind.

Sparkle on, O waves, and thou breeze behind us blow into the open bay, where even now my night quarters can be seen afar off.

This was, indeed, a pleasant sail. The hotel at Motala was very easy to find, and only a few yards from the lake; but the number of people who had observed the Rob Roy approaching (always more noticeable when its pure white sails are spread) gave me a constant stream of visitors, respectful, but inquisitive to an unusual degree.

The venerable landlady became fired with the desire to see the start next day.

She leant upon my arm, walking to the water—a dame of lady-like mien, with that waxen imperishable tint of cheek which hale old age has sometimes—and you may defy paint to imitate this bloom.

On the bridge a beggar accosted me, and I fairly started with surprise. The thing was so new—this was the first and last beggar we met in our tour.

O rich England! rouse up and relieve poor ragged Englishmen. The squalid poverty in our wealthy land is oppressive; the fat riches in it are oppressive. Thousands of the poor in London never see a rich man's smile of sympathy, or hear his voice to cheer them. Thousands of rich men never see the misery of the poor, or hear their cry of hunger. The rich and poor among us are too distinct by class and locality. They may have liberty to live far apart as west from east; but cannot we urge by love, or must we force by law the fulness of the one to help the wan emptiness of the other?

This highly respectable Svenske beggar, however, pleaded in such gentlemanly tones that I gave him a great polygon of copper, which weighed heavy in my pocket, and would be too heavy for the canoe. The coin puzzled the man, and it puzzled his friends when he showed it to them, and he and they burst into merry laughter, for they thought it was a joke of the paddler—a grim joke, indeed, to play on a polite mendicant!

The Motala River, as it rushes out of Vettern to run through a chain of lakes, and by devious ways to the Baltic, is seized upon at once, that it may yield some of its water-power to everybody on the banks, and so there is a network of barriers, dams, sluices, forces, falls, weirs, and rapids, with a ceaseless splashing sound, and the rap-ap-ap of busy waterwheels, and clang of great hammers, and hoarse hissing of swift saws, all mingled with the hum and bustle of many men at work, an exceedingly interesting exhibition of picturesque industry.

The great ironworks of Motala we had visited with much curiosity ten years ago, but they have been largely improved and extended since that time. The new requirements of modern warfare are met by private energy in a great company like this at Motala, and there are the massive plates are rolled for the Monitor steamers. Two of these were already afloat. The Motala company has another branch elsewhere, and a third at Norrköping, where the third Monitor was seen just ready for launching, as will be described further on. The turret of one of the Monitors, to hold two guns, was set up in the yard, and the workmanship of the whole was admirable. In such work the managers have a rule not to hurry any of the men. They prefer that time should be spent, even more than what is reasonable, rather than have one stroke of the hammer hasty or neglected. When the Yankee Mianontomoh came to Stockholm to astonish the Swedes, she was received by their far better vessels; for in iron-works, and with a Swedish engineer like Ericcson to direct them, Sweden ought not to be easily distanced.

Here also, we saw a Swedish gunboat, very like a canoe in shape; indeed, the Rob Roy was carried into the building-yard and placed beside its enormous fellow of the waters, to the great amusement of the workmen and of myself.

That this likeness between the iron giant and the oaken pigmy was no mere fancy will be seen by a glance at the drawing; from which it appears that the gunboat slopes down, fore and aft, from a higher centre, and is covered on deck, and so formed as to go through and under the waves;

PARVO COMPONERE MAGNUM.

while most vessels are built to go over them, or, at least, to make the attempt.

Only one gun is on this terrible war ship, and as it cannot be "trained" or moved athwartships, the whole vessel has to be steered so as to direct the gun. The boat is about 100 feet long, so that it can cross Sweden through the locks.

After showing me all that was to be seen here, the gentleman in charge kindly gave me a written permission to pass free of expense through all the canal locks. But as it is the prerogative of the Rob Roy never to go through any locks, but always to take a little country walk round about them instead, it seemed at first as if this paper would be of no use.

Not so. Passing on our way until the time came for the mid-day meal, we pulled up at a lock-keeper's house, knocked, and went in. Two women were seated there, and a baby. "Can you give me milk?" (The first time I had ever asked for such a luxury with my chocolate). No answer. "Any bread?" Still dumb. They gave no attention whatever. They had not seen the boat. They thought I was a tramp. I then produced the paddle, and they were puzzled, nay, appalled. Soothing the frightened baby with some sugar, and presenting a paper full of pictures to its grandmother, I coolly set up my spirit-stove on their table, and commenced the cooking in a most methodical manner. Their mingled amazement and curiosity was highly amusing; but I kept my countenance gravely, and then handed them the magic paper of orders to the lock-keepers. A great change at once began, and all was bustle; but I got no milk. They looked hard at the paper, which inspired all the more awe because they could not read a word of it (in writing) until a man came in, and then a wonderful jabbering of tongues began, and went on all through my dinner; and it may be going on still.

Many English canoeists, several of them members of the

Canoe Club, have paddled over Scandinavia since the Rob Roy tried that pleasant cruising ground. All these wanderers seem to have been well received, and from one and another, at intervals, I obtain pleasant news of the various personages mentioned in our log.

## END NOTES

1—The use of gas is rapidly spreading in Sweden. English coals can be had here as cheaply as in the south of England, for they come in vessels that take back wood. Indeed, English coal is used on all the steamers and railways, even where millions of trees are waiting to be cut down. At Helsingborg we noticed a man digging coal out of the bank at the side of his house, and at the same time a fleet of English colliers was sailing past in the Sound.

# CHAPTER VIII

Washing Day — Feeding on Tin — Horse Steak — Queer
College — Choosing Partners — Laborious Wedding —
That Tiresome Wire — Roxen Locks — Murdered Tongue
— Observation — Solus — Lone Happiness.

THIS was washing day on board the ship Rob Roy
(Wednesday and Saturday were always so); therefore it
was important to have fine drying weather.

On such an occasion all hands were piped on deck by
the boatswain at an early hour; and the last pair that came
up were told off to "scrub ship and wash clothes." All
these articles were then put out to dry on the boom, where
they dangled in the sun and the breeze, quite regardless of
the public opinion or otherwise of landlubbers ashore.

It was the duty, of course, of the mate to make a correct
list of the washing, and to enter the same in the log.[1]

When it was necessary to wash the sails of the canoe
(to maintain her respectable character under critical
examination), this had to be done during her stay in some
port, while she was dismantled for a time, and the crew
had shore leave.

Then the sails were sent to a regular washerwoman;
and their shape, size, and material puzzled her very much,
so that she came herself with smiles to return them to the
captain, washed white as snow, and ironed in squares like
a table-cloth, with the list pinned on them—"One suit of

sails, with tacks, leaches, sheets, grommets, and halyards attached."

A small store of provisions, and a mild effort to cook them, were two features added to the voyage, after the sharp experience of jejune days last year on the Danube, where the only thing in the eating line that was always ready was "Hunger Sauce." But the head cook of the Rob Roy was an ignoramus in his art. His essays were humble failures; and he trusted his guests to enjoy rather the circumstances and poetry of the repast, than the delicacies thereof.

It was a rule always to carry food for one day's hard eating, or two days of meagre diet. Biscuits kept well all the way round, and some have survived to this hour. A small bottle of brandy was refilled every week from the "reserve stores" (sent in advance), until all the English brandy was done, and then foreign brandy had to be added to the little remnant of true British smack; just as new planks, and then a new keel, are put into an old ship, but it is always felt to be the "old ship" still.

The spirit-stove for cooking, which had been procured in Oxford Street, with all due heralding of its perfections, had its failings too, and, moreover, had to be sheltered from wind during its use; but then there was plenty of wood, in dry days, for an open fire; and the lively crackling of blazing logs made it well worth the little trouble of hauling them through the dense thickets.

Our cook's first attempt to make an oatmeal cake was certainly most disheartening; some people, indeed, cannot eat this excellent Scottish diet, but at any rate all cannot make it. He mixed the water and oatmeal, and had a round tin-plate heating on the flame, whereon the mixture was poured. It steamed, it set, it dried hard; and then he removed the plate from the fire, but alas! the cake would not come off the tin-plate till it was torn away with struggles and a knife; and then all the lower part of the brown cake was covered with bright tin, and it had to be thrown away with a sigh, and gone was my only hope of breakfast; for even sea air does not enable you to digest sheet tin.

Practice taught by hunger improved the cuisine steadily, and in a rough way we soon learned to put smoking soup on the table, stirring the bread, rice, or biscuits into it with the long wooden spoon, which is narrow at the end, so as to do for eggs also. Chocolate succeeded well, and tea and coffee; and the crew soon became accustomed to eat raw fish when they saw other people eating it with gusto; just as in Russia one carves away comfortably at a tough hind leg of a horse, but in England we should, on the whole, prefer a sirloin of beef.

Of course it is often, though by no means always, feasible to carry from the house you stop at for the night a good supply for dinner of bread and meat and eggs, and sometimes wine; but the addition of something hot, which the stomach craves for after hours of exhausting exercise, cannot, I think, be withheld for many days without impairing that full and hearty vigour without which a voyage of this sort must be rather a poor sort of treat.[1]

Now we have discussed the viands, and the steward of the Rob Roy packs the boxes and parcels and machinery of them carefully into a neat little basket, fitting under deck behind my back; and as our subject is done, and our cigar, it is time to shove off again into the water, rested, fed, and with sentiments to all mankind most bland.

At the end of the canal there were more locks, descending to the Boren Lake, but these the boat ran past, merrily gliding down hill on a grassy slope. Then we hoisted sail to a fine strong favourable breeze, and sped fast away in the most lively fashion, visiting all parts of the lake, and loth to allow that the end was reached at last. Again into a canal, long and rather weary, compared with the dancing billowets of the lake, but clean, deep, wide, and winding, with fish leaping and birds singing; in fact, as good as a canal could be.

At the end of a long day it was a wonder we had not come to our destination, a place called Berg, but not visible from the canal. However, we came to a lock, and three boys came to look on, and then at least fifty youths, all dressed with white neckties; so we concluded it must be some sort of college; but it was surprising to find that not one of the students could speak German, French, Italian, or Latin. Though greatly puzzled, it was needful to find night quarters; so we bore the canoe off to a large house in mirthful procession. Here we found a considerable hubbub in progress, and a tray laid out with about fifty glasses of punch on it.

It struck me that the rations, or "commons," of the college were more liberal than their linguistic accomplishments; but the punch was excellent, and a man dressed in military uniform, who I concluded was the drill-master, pressed me to enter and be at home. All right.

Presently there came one who had been sent for and could talk French, and then all the mysterious riddle was explained. I had come just in time for the wedding-supper of the daughter of the wealthy landlord, and all these dressed-up collegians were only his friends accoutred for the evening party; and as boys (not to say men) usually find marriage feasts to be very dull proceedings after an hour or two, the delight of these youngsters at the interlude of a canoe arrival may be imagined.

The only place for me to sleep in was an anteroom with a sofa in it; and even this room was held as a fortress by the butler for his stock of beer and wine, and it was not vacated until one o'clock in the morning. As well as a tired paddler could, I joined the "Borrullup," as this feast is called, and a young lady was introduced who could speak English, they said—but not one word could she recollect. In preference I gave my arm to one of the bridesmaids, and led her down to supper, and she seemed very well pleased with the "Engelsman" who came in a boat, so we had a lively conversation, each of us in our own language, quite independently. The supper was a most stupid affair, all people standing, and with long intervals between hot courses of strong food, suitable for the midday hours, perhaps, but quite *de trop* at midnight. Several speeches were made, and healths proposed by the gentleman in uniform, one of the "best men" of the bridegroom—for he has a subdivision here, to help him to carry his cares. Now and then I slipped off to lie down and rest on my sofa, amid the bottles, which were numerous and speedily emptied, and when the happy pair presented themselves, as is the custom, at the window for the inspection of a crowd outside, who had long been gazing through the lower panes in silent and rapt awe at the splendour of the bridal lace, I thought it a good move to exhibit my magnesium-wire light, which was just the right thing in the right place, for it lit up all the hillside, and showed a hundred faces, all turned one way, with one look of admiring wonder on all, and one hue of ghastly paleness.

It is really amusing to think how many separate crowds of people in various countries have been illuminated and delighted by the little half yard of wire given to me last year on the lake of Zug by and English friend I met there. Some inches of the pretty metal remain even now to make some hundreds gape.

The crowd gathered early to start the Rob Roy next day upon the beautiful Lake Roxen, of which I had to traverse the full length. The canal approaches close to the lake, but about seventy feet above it, and the usual descent is by eleven locks; but as they are close together, the canoe had merely to slide down the grass sloping to the verge of the water. A large party of people happened then to be coming up the ascent, while their steamer would be delayed two hours or more in passing the locks; and a

good deal of amusement was afforded to them by seeing the swift traverse of the Rob Roy over the grass.

The weather was superb, and I sailed about in the lake wasting time rather imprudently, for it was only eighteen miles long, if we had kept the proper course. Near the end of the day, and as the shores approached closer together, the navigation became so complicated, and the islands and bays so confused, that I went down a wrong channel; therefore all the labour of the past had to be done three times instead of once, and vainly still I searched for the village of Norsholm. But the weather was lovely, and only too hot when the wind died down, and that soft mild calm of the setting sun, which lasts so long here, refreshed my tired limbs. At last I found a lady and gentleman in a boat fishing, and when I asked where I could sleep that night, the man pointed to a Louse. Let me write what was said, just to show how few words of Swedish will do, and how very badly even these may be spoken and yet be enough. "Min Herr, jag ar Engelsk; var kan jag liga i nat? jag önskar sofva." That is intended to mean, "Sir, I am English; where can I sleep to-night? I want a bed." Speedily he asked me to his own house, a pretty villa just by the water, and there this kind Mr. Carlman and his young wife were my hospitable entertainers. He could speak English, and had read of the Rob Roy in the papers, and, indeed, he was as pleased as I was with our *rencontre*.

Mrs. Carlman curtsied deep when I gave her a little paper in Swedish, and the "British Workman" was for her husband. A number of copies of this excellent periodical are now adorning the walls of Swedish inns and private houses; and I think it would be a good plan if the woodcuts used for it could be lent to some one in Sweden, who might republish the periodical in the Swedish language.[2]

Here, then, we are well housed for the night; and how lucky the paddler has been in coming always to friendly hosts, so that, with the exception of the first night in Norway, passed in wakeful irritation on the bed of straw, we have, in one way or another, been comfortably lodged every night.

The common pleasures of travelling may be agreeably varied, when your journey is among a people who are strange enough to be worth observing in themselves as men and women; so that not only the scenery, but what is done and what is said by fellow-beings round enlists attention.

After much travelling in our own country, we at least

seem to know all that the people around us will say or do; at any rate enough to be tired of its study, if a wet day keeps us in from the hills and dales of Nature.

But dropping as a tourist into a remote district of Sweden, or on a sea-girt isle of Denmark, you have at once a pleasant curiosity to see the manners of the new people, and an eager desire to find out what they are saying, and yet were it all understood or translated, the spell of curiosity might be broken, if you found the unknown talk was dull.

Travelling alone is the only way to enjoy this simple pleasure of quiet regarding. For if you travel with a companion you will speak to him, and lose what others are saying; and if both you and your fellow-tourist are silent, the people about you perceive at once you are observing them. Then they become non-natural. They are now actors only, and the charm of the scene is spoiled. For observing the manners, and for learning the language, for sketching, for writing, for reflecting, and for reading, as well as for temper and freedom, and a special *un*named sentimental enjoyment of the incidents abroad, the traveller must travel alone. But as nobody will do this because another says he likes to do it, we shall not hope now to convince or persuade, but we merely record what all will certify who have made good trial of a solitary tour.

The enjoyment of lone travel is intensified by voyaging in a canoe, for this isolates more completely than any other mode. During the working hours of the day the want of a companion is never felt, because every moment has engagement for the mind in searching the way and managing the boat; and if in fishing, too, why, for *that*, it is confessed on all hands that to enjoy it thoroughly you must be alone. Arrived with the canoe at evening, and healthfully tired, what is it you want most? If chatter, then there are plenty of visitors ready. But what the body now wants most is rest at full length on the top of a bed, and the mind, too, wants rest in a new attitude of thought. A "pleasant and lively companion" would be just the thing *not* to give pleasure then, but a pleasant book will.

All this we had enjoyed and appreciated in many former tours; but in the present voyage there is the still closer isolation of the solitary bivouac.

A fire of sticks on the ground out of doors—does it not remind us of schoolboy days, when a half-holiday looked as long as a week does now? As a boy one had uproarious enjoyment in a bonfire, and in the roasted potatoes from its white-ashed embers. Yet as a man and at home one could scarcely feed thus in a field, unless with a nice party of friends, when the affair at once becomes a picnic, and is dependent on far other elements for its being tolerably pleasant. But sail you over the seas, prosaic man, a thousand miles away from home, from friends, from all men, and all women; away from houses, horses, cows, carts, hedges, bridges, and even from ships. Peel off the last circumstance of civilization; and when all this husk is off there will bud forth freshly from the untramelled inner mind a new and tender flower of rare beauty and enjoyment—unless, indeed, yours is a poor suffocated soul—*the delight of being alone.*

Seek out a shady bank, on a thick wooded isle, in a rocky nook by the deep clear water, and on a summer day; there it will spring up, that quite new sentiment—too delicate to be shared by another, for it is broken if divided, and it is lost like water spilled, and so a mere bubble, perhaps, but still, if untouched, it is full, complete, and beautiful. Enough has now been said to recall this feeling, if you have ever known it. If you have not, my pen, less practised than my paddle, is too clumsy to paint the unknown. A feeble enjoyment of this new sensation may be slightly felt when your only companion is a foreign guide—a Swiss in the Alps, a Kabyle in the Atlas, or an

Indian in the prairie—and then only just in proportion as he is obtuse, silent, or asleep, and so is most like an animal, or, better, like a stone. Even then the unseen and ignored companion may spoil it all by suddenly becoming present; he may awake, or alas ! he may *snore*, or the sound may come through the tent of your horse munching his beans; and away flies the fairy sentiment, which cannot endure even the bleating of a lamb on a far-off hill. Your flower will close his petals, and your bubble will be burst. You are no longer alone.

The rill of pleasure from this source once set flowing in the canoe tour will be an undercurrent for weeks, and will trickle through the mind sweetly in a stream without form or boundary, or will gush up at times with an aroma of thought—the dream of a dream, in visions that a Tennyson can tell in words, but all can grasp and feel. This current will also gather force enough to bear the checks of occasional town life and hotels; but it is revelled in most fully as a deep pool of pleasure after the solitary, silent bivouac, when the prosaic body itself becomes as if absent, ruminating; and the wondrous thing called "Mind," feeling the silence round, creeps forth, at first stealthily; but now, being assured that no one sees or hears, and nothing else is near, and that there is freedom to unfold in, it slowly rises, erect, awake, a majestic form, awful, incomprehensible.

Then begin the grand gymnastics of this giant unbound—the far-reaching stretches into the long past, but grasping only emptiness; the anxious gropings into the deep below, in vain; and then the nimble plays of fancy round the near and present; and, still unsatisfied, and craving still for what is lasting and true, it bounds off into the dim future, soon dashing against a wall of hard, cold darkness, firm and impenetrable.

Stay, weary spirit, and at last look *up*, and listen to that solemn voice, "Be still, and know that I am God." "Faithful and true;" "that liveth, and was dead;" "the Everlasting Father, the Prince of Peace;" and so you are *not* alone.

## END NOTES
1—These lists were not dissimilar, nor were they voluminous. The following is a copy of the longest ever known : — "List of washing — One sock, one pocket-handkerchief another sock, the collar."
2—This has since been done not only for Sweden but for France and Spain, and the "Children's Friend" in Arabic is now on every table and in many dark houses of the Druse villages of Mount Lebanon.

# CHAPTER IX.

Poke the Fire — Flies and Flies — Sport and Play — Won't give in — Breakers!— Bivouac — Surgeon's Report — Search for a Town — Norrköping Falls — Rest.

DAWN — time to rise after a good sleep in a pleasant room. Many of these rooms, however, which appear so comfortable in summer because they are light and airy and large, must be very different to live in when the mercury is low zero in the cold winter nights.

The use of a closed stove in foreign countries, instead of an open fire-place, as in England, at once reminds the traveller that he is away from home.

Doubtless the stove is more economical and more philosophical, and it will keep all parts of a room equally warm; whereas our wasteful grate only heats one side of everything; and you may be slowly roasted at one end of the table, while your best friend is frozen at the other.

Yet there are few of us, indeed, who would surrender the open coal fire and its glowing hearth and soft warm rug, even though we have to gather round closely, and must stoop to enjoy its one-sided warmth.

The difference between the modes of heating the houses of Englishmen and Swedes is not unlike that between their two countries as regards wealth, refinement, and education; for while in England we have a thousand very rich and a thousand very poor, a thousand highly refined and a thousand very brutal, a thousand learned men and a thousand utterly ignorant, there seems to be in Norway and Sweden a general moderate competence, a sufficient courtesy, and a fair education throughout the whole.

But it is summer still, so we need not sit round the fire for a chat. Let us stroll down to the water's edge, and rig up the fishing-rod, and seek out the best flies from our book, for it looks like fisherman's weather.

And with regard to this sport of fishing, it certainly was a grand addition now to the pleasures of last year's voyage, though we had scarcely prepared sufficiently for its proper enjoyment In the lakes fish are caught best with the minnow and the trolling-line, being dainty animals that like to dine methodically, and to begin by eating fish. As for the artificial fly, their ignorance of its satisfying sweetness is lamentable. They regard it as only a kickshaw, or, at most, it will do for dessert.

We had not been warned of this, and so had brought only flies; and as trolling-hooks could not be procured until the best lakes for using them were passed, it was only in the rivers that we had profitable sport, for sport it is even to fish without catching; and the man who fishes for the fishes, and not for the fishing, is not a true fisherman.

Also let me say that the fishing-laws are not good ones in these parts; moreover, the people do not keep them. Even in some of the most famed fishing-grounds we found that fish are now very scarce, and are more expensive for food than butcher's meat. After fishing very carefully over one very good-looking lake, I was told at the end that not one single fish had ever been heard of there. So I think now a really good case has been made out in defense of my having only small sport, and seldom; and was there ever a fisherman who had not most weighty reasons for a light basket?

Still, it was great fun thus fishing; and even when you

cannot feel every moment that a ten-pounder is just about to rise, there is some satisfaction in being able to flog the water.

So hie away in the beauteous morn, and before the sleepy rolling mist has risen from the lake. But there was an evident stream here; and I renewed the old and pleasant sensation experienced on the Rhine last year, in shooting right ahead through perfectly white fog. The ear would have easily told of any serious difficulty in the way, so it was tolerably safe and very amusing.

When the sun did burst through, we began at once with a lucky red hackle, for the river seemed good for a fish or two.

Casting my fly behind a great rock, it was taken by a fish, and I saw very soon he was a large one. He played in the most puzzling manner for half-an-hour—often jumping out of the water, and often dragging the boat near

" LED BY THE NOSE."

rocks and rapids; but I would have sooner jumped into the water than lose such a prize. Three times he got under the boat, and I feared then for the thin line against the iron keel, What with the fish, the paddle, the rocks and trees and the current, I once got so entangled that my rod slipped out of my hand; but it had no reel on, so it floated, and we gave chase up the stream, and caught and grasped the butt once more—the fish still on. My little landing net was not ready. Indeed, I was not quite prepared for so good a take all at once (fishermen will understand this state of things); so the manner of getting him into the boat was the real point of puzzle. Twice I had my macintosh apron under him, but failed to secure his cold, flat, slippery sides, until at the third attempt, when I fairly shovelled him into the boat, with a deluge of water—a nine-pound grayling, and well worth all the time and trouble, as every sportsman will allow.

It is evident, however, that to fish in a small canoe, when you manage the sails, the paddle, and the rod with only two hands, and when you have to attend to the wind, the current, and your flies, is a full tax on energy, and needs great attention; and it was well to put on the cork-seat life-preserver when fishing in the deep lakes and sailing at the same time, because one might be entangled then among the ropes and strings and fishing-line, if an upset were to occur.

The banks of "Motala Ström" equalled all we had heard in their praise; and it was quite a pleasure to feel how much was gained by the detour I was now making for scenery's sake. For at Norsholm the canal leaves Lake Roxen to go east to Söderköping, whereas the River Motala turns due north, and will soon bring us into a large lake, quite out of the usual beat, and by which we can reach Norrköping.

Beautiful villas, meadows, gardens, orchards, and mills were scattered along shady reaches of quiet water or by bubbling pools and steep rocky hollows. At length a loud rushing sound roused me, as the well-known signal of "breakers ahead." This was a waterfall, too deep, high, and furious to pass in any boat; and the men from a sawmill near all ran to see the canoe when we stopped to reconnoitre.

"This is from England," said I; and the master answered "Ya." Thereby it was plain he had read all about her in his newspaper, else he would have replied, "So — o — o ? ? ?" as they invariably do when they mean our "Indeed?"

His men helped me; and they rejoiced much to receive the grayling as a present in return; for the fish was too heavy to carry further, and we had still thirty miles to do.

A little tired with the morning's work, and with eleven hours in the boat on the preceding day, I now sought a shady cave by the water for a good long "dine." Here you might see the canoe drawn up in a spot which seems perfect for a bivouac, and all the boat's stores displayed, with plenty of dry wood at hand, and a good dry rock to cook upon. There was but one defect in all this arrangement—but that was a fatal one—the water was not clear.

It was at the *embouchure* of the river, and only half-a-mile from the turbulence of the cascade, and not far enough into the lake to allow the troubled mud to subside. Although this dirty water was soon noticed, we were too lazy to pack up and go on a few miles, and to begin again; therefore, in a bad compromise the cook was ordered to make chocolate, as if by its luscious flavour we could sweeten the green water.

The palate may be trifled with, but in a voyage of this sort the stomach will stand no nonsense. Forced to work hard all day, this important department insists on good food, or it will "strike."

Mine struck with all its powers, combining "as one

man;" but the food was forced down amid the general discontent of the community, and the bivouac was converted into a pitched battle between the mind that insisted on feeding and the body that refused to be fed with mud-cocoa.

A victory for the hour by the party of force, just as in the body politic, may result only in the prostration of all parties afterwards ; and so it was, for the beauties of Lake Glan now spread out before the eyes in vain; birds warbled, but the ear heeded not, and to all sweet odours the nose was disdainfully turned up. Though we sailed, fished, paddled, whistled, and sung, there was a dull heavy sickness under all the forced mirth. The surgeon of the Rob Roy hereby warns all paddlers to beware of doubtful water, when they mean to work long in the sun, and their lot is cast in a cholera land.

Well, enjoyment came again, nevertheless, in the evening, as of yore, and, after many a tack while the wind lasted, and full many a stroke with the paddle, at last we neared the end of the lake, where, according to the map, you will see that Norrköping ought to be—and pray be good enough to call it Norchipping.

But this shy town resolutely stayed behind a hill, and with my best efforts I could not discover the way to it. A man passed in a boat and shouted out, and a number of his vowels reached me; but after half-an-hour's threading through weeds and islands in the direction he advised, it was only too plain that he had been showing how to go to Norrköping by land; so I had to hark back and begin the whole affair again, while the light was fading and the Rob Roy was weary.

Then our boatswain had to go ashore, and to mount several islands, one after another, for a view; but the intricacy seemed only more entangled each time it was scanned, for not one outlet could be seen to any of the arms of the lake.

Much of the difficulty in finding the way, both on Roxen and Glan, was owing to the inaccuracy of the map—not the excellent map brought from London (for that did not extend to these two lakes), but another, bought at Vadstena, and highly recommended as "new, cheap, and good." I can only say that it had straight coasts where there were twenty bends, and that no island was depicted on it unless it was half an inch long. Such a map is quite useless for lakes like the two we have just been lost upon.

It is needless to detail all the devices we had to practise to extricate the Rob Roy from its labyrinth, and for which it was necessary to ascertain the slight but perceptible motion of a current at the end of Lake Glan. This, at last, was only done by watching those indescribable signs which the canoeist learns to know, as an Indian discerns a trail where no one else can see it, even if it is pointed out.

But I shall not forget the pleasure of finding at length the sought-for outlet, and there was even satisfaction (that of "No wonder I could not!") in perceiving how very unusual was its form, bent round at right angles, hidden from view, and looking so very innocent all the time. Then came a pleasant current, and all was life in my crew, though they had been on the stretch again for eleven hours, and there were several miles yet to be done.

It will be understood that no attempt is made in our log to record the various separate lakes of smaller dimensions we passed through, and the still more numerous ponds, like the Serpentine, though these were often pretty and interesting, but a mere list of them would not be at all so. However, the Motala Ström became now again a downright river, and asserted its right to run, and resumed its attractive beauty. Villas and deep groves and avenues were on the banks, high and richly-wooded, while the water was clean and deep, until we came to the falls at Norrköping so suddenly that I had to hurry from mid-stream to the bank, where a man was fishing with a net. He said no man could be had there to carry my boat; and, as this was quite a new answer to the usual question, we landed to inspect the place, the man following, rather solemn in mood, and a good deal taken aback at the sudden intrusion. I found I had come ashore in the premises of a prison for females, and hence the man's refusal to help the proceeding!

It is often thus that some apparent incivility may be only the result of causes we do not appreciate until after examination. But I was now in a great difficulty. The stream was too strong for me to reascend in my tired condition, and the question was, shall I be able to cross to the other side, on the verge of this great fall, without much danger of being carried over? After spying from various quarters, and well considering the matter, I felt sure it was to be done, provided every stroke of the paddle were to be a true one, and made to tell; and then, bracing up my tired muscles, and after a short pull at some brandy (only useful for very momentary work like this), I shot across like an arrow; and soon the Rob Roy reclined at rest in the coach-house of a fine hotel at Norrköping.

We rested a day here (August 24), for, in spite of my determination over and over again not to work too hard, I had been far too long in my journeys every day for some time past; and though at the time one's spirit and the great excitement and pleasure of paddling and sailing may enable great exertion to be undergone, it is sure to prove too much when continued for many days, and especially if the hours of sleep are contracted or disturbed, and the meals are irregular and often meagre besides.

Here, then, emerging from the maze of inland waters, and now upon the shores of the Baltic Sea, it may be allowed to pause a little, and draw breath.

"O, land! thou land of thousand lakes,

Of song and constancy;
Against whose strand life's ocean breaks,
Where dreams the past, the future wakes :
Oh, blush not for thy poverty,
Be hopeful, bold, and free !
Thy blossom in the bud that lies
Shall burst its fetters strong;
Lo ! from our tender love shall rise
Thy light, thy fame, thy hopes, thy joys;
And prouder far shall sound, ere long,
Our Finland's patriot song!"
[*From "Vort Land" a Scandinavian Song by Runeberg.*]

# CHAPTER X.

Right about Face — Another revolution — A Radical Tory —
Boys' Beadle — You shall teach — On the Baltic — Maps —
Launched — Fog at Sea — Man in the Mist — A Night Peril
— Stockholm.

IN the passage across Sweden during the last three
weeks, I had met with no parasol, no chimney-pot hat, no
funeral, no blow given in anger, no fight, no quarrel, no
carpet, no cripple, no idiot, one man running, one soldier,
one who could not read, one beggar, one blind man, one
insane, one very handsome man, and how many pretty girls I
will not tell you.

Why, we must have been quite out of society there?

That is a matter of opinion, and the facts are before you.

As for the "one man running," it is exclusive of the
people who ran to see the Rob Roy; for in fact the Swedes do
not exhibit much agility, being a sedate comfortable people;
and one wonders what their manly exercises are.

However, in the upper part of Vermland, and in the
district of Norway near it, there is a very strange physical feat
sometimes practised, which is also known in many parts of
Scotland. One day when two friends were walking with me
in a sequestered part of Norway, we heard a curious sound
on the other side of a dike, which was first a great smack, as
if something had thumped the ground, and then a puffing
and blowing of somebody breathing hard and quickly.

"SALMON POLKA."

On approaching the place we saw over the fence a young man quite alone, who was practising over and over the most inexplicable leap into the air that could be devised for human body. He swang himself up, and then round on his head for a point, when his upper leg described a great circle, and came down at last with a resounding whack.

Inquiry about the gymnastic performance is answered by telling me that it is an ancient dance-step of that region, and is called in Swedish "Giesse Härad Polska," that is, "Salmon-district step;" perhaps the first dancing-master who taught it learned the leap from a salmon.

Norrköping reminded me of some of the towns on the Danube, where the river is banked up to work numerous wheels, and there is a gushing, rushing, splashing sound all day and all night, with waterfall spray rising slowly in the morning air.

There is a railway here, and a large hotel, business in the streets, and a huge cloth-mill peering over the Motala, where it makes its last few noisy leaps, tumbling over rocks into the Baltic, to be lost in the great sea.

As we are not professing to describe foreign lands and towns and the people in them, but only to write the log of a canoe, it will hardly do to give an account here of the politics or education of Sweden, though both of these are very interesting; the first, because a wonderful change has just been effected in the mode of government—a revolution complete but bloodless; and the second, because the system of education, for the masses at least, appears to be the most successful in the world.

Sweden, until last summer, had four houses in its legislature—nobles, clerics, burgesses, and landowners. Two of these houses are abolished, the nobles surrendering their special privileges as hereditary legislators, and the clergy vacating their special priestly chamber. Now there are two Houses of Parliament only, to which any man may be sent, without reference to his trade or business, by the votes of electors widely enfranchised.

On the Upper and Lower House, then, and on the king, as a third leg of the stool, rests the seat of government; and probably its base will be as stable on three legs as on five. The first elections under the new system were proceeding during my visit, and it was curious to observe the coy delicacy with which men handled the untried engine of power.

For example, a friend of mine desired to get into the Lower House (as better for action and spirited debate), but his neighbours wished to elect him as a member of the Upper and more dignified body. Now, by the new law, he must not canvass, and he must not even issue a proposal as candidate. Perhaps, then, by this time he is a Senator against his will.[1] Time will work this stiffness off, alas! and no doubt, in a few years, there will be election "lambs," even by the green shores of Vettern.

A banker here, Mr. E— , was very kind to me; and gave a sumptuous dinner to the crew of the Rob Roy, where we met two other gentlemen, who could speak English. After this, perhaps, it is unfair to tell the political creed of our host—a Tory, who wishes to see women sitting (he did not actually say, *speaking*) in Parliament. Mr. Stuart Mill is, therefore, outbid entirely—for I suppose he only likes feminine electors; but it would, indeed, be worth while being an M.P. oneself to see the Chancellor of the Exchequer badgered on an amendment by Dr. Emma Blew, Memberess for Honiton.

On a beautiful hill near the town are the new State schools. The buildings are large and handsome, airy and light, and with gardens round, where the children are permitted to work if very good at their lessons. The scholars comprise many who would be in our Ragged-schools, and who do not pay for their education. Every child in Sweden above six years old must learn to read, or if not, a policeman brings him to school; but there is little need of such compulsion, for a person employed in each district goes to all refractory parents and persuades them to comply with the useful rule.[2] No child may be employed in a factory until he is twelve years old, and has learned, at any rate, the *minimum* of ordinary education. The school-rooms are admirably furnished—maps and pictures enliven the walls, and a gymnasium and playground vary the scene. At each desk sit two pupils, each with a chair adjusted to his height, and with excellent arrangements for desks and school furniture, being the same as won the first prize when Sweden exhibited them at our London Exhibition of 1862. There are twenty-five women teachers, and only four men. The influence of men by command is said to be less useful than that of women by their gentleness and grace; but all the teachers are carefully selected, "because the worst materials need the best instruments to work upon them." The whole plan and scope of the system seems very like that in America; and it is within the power of a small town to adopt and to perfect machinery of this kind, when a few active men like the Swedish banker can be interested enough to manage it. Still, after numerous visits to foreign schools and large experience of our own, I cannot say "No" to the question, "Is it wrong to compel every child living in our land to learn, when we insist upon it in our own homes? And may we not punish a father who starves his child's mind, when we may punish him if he starves its body?" The crew of the Rob Roy, on being polled, decided by a casting vote in favour of compulsory education.[3]

A little way down the river, we next went to visit quite another sort of Monitors—those with the iron-sides—of which one designed by the Swede-American Ericcson lies here ready to be launched. It is a huge, ugly, and impenetrable thing, perfectly fitted for its fearful purpose, and horribly suggestive of crashing shells and thundering blows, and the shouts and shrieks of war.

But let us return to our own peaceful boat, as the poet beautifully says:

"Robur et æs triplex,
    Qui primus;"

and the other poet beautifully renders:

"The Rob Roy, first (of oak) canoed a trip at ease,
    By paddle, sail, and cart, through forest, lake, and seas."

For this page of the log will recount the first trip on the Baltic Sea by our little canoe, after three weeks spent most pleasantly on the inland "Sees," and lesser lakes, and broad rivers, and purling streams of Norway and Sweden. It was natural enough for me to wish for a paddle on the veritable sea waves, though those on Venern are sometimes quite as large, and the surge on Lake Vettern is more trying to muscle and pluck, with its sharp pointed crests, when a south wind blows.

To give me a good long day in the open sea, I arranged

with a steamer to take us along the winding estuary of the Broviken, until she had to turn south-east on her course, and there to drop me in the waves, to paddle and sail north-east for Stockholm.

Crowds gathered to see the canoe on the deck of the "Gotha," and a regular stream of visitors came up one stairs and went down the other, pacing slowly round the little craft, peering into it, measuring with tapes and foot-rules, lifting it, patting it, rubbing it, and then always settling on the flag; but at that point the marine on duty always said "paws off," which the Swedes will hereafter understand means "don't touch." They were amused to see me lay in provisions for three days (of course, on very short rations), so that if the west wind then blowing should increase, and by any accident we might be blown off land, our little shipload would possibly reach the Russian coast, at any rate.

Oddly enough, not two of the visitors agreed as to whether the water of the Baltic is too salt to drink. Probably it is in some parts very much salter than in others, but we arranged this matter by saying it would do for salt soup, and I also took a bottle of sherry to make sure. The harbourmaster was on board the steamer—an old sailor, and constantly cruising about these coasts—so we got full directions where to steer for by the steamer's chart, though all efforts to get a proper compass were unsuccessful.

In the Danube voyage last year, it was found that the frequent reference necessary to a map made it advisable to cut the large map into small squares, so that, when used on service, no unfolding was required, and only a small part (showing about three days' journey) was exposed to the rain, wind, and vicissitudes of canoe life, while the reference-square was conveniently carried in the pocket.

This arrangement was now matured, so that on the last voyage I carried in my breast-pocket a piece of cardboard doubled, and showing, when opened, one square of map and one square of blank paper. Both of these were constantly

**Map 3.**

**ROUTE OF THE BOB ROY**
in
**DENMARK, SLESVIC,**
**HOLSTEIN & THE NORTH SEA.**
indicated by a dotted line.

used—the one to get information from, and the other to note observations on with a pencil.

One of these map-squares is reproduced as Map 3, but only some of the numerous rivers, lakes, and names upon the original map (those nearer the canoe route) are printed in the copy.

It will be observed that the route on this map, through part of Vermland, comprises one long day's voyage from Arvika to Higsitter, a short day's march while carting the boat to Borgivik, and a third day's winding pull on Venern round to Carlstadt. This is the largest scale of map to be procured (costing 24*s*. in London), but still only about one island in every five will be found marked upon it.

It may seem strange to a boating man that there should be any difficulty in finding the course when one has a good map and good weather; but it has been already explained that the islands constitute the chief difficulty, and in most places the inhabitants, and especially the sailors, expressed great surprise that a canoe could find its way in these archipelagoes at all. No part of the coast of Europe that I have seen, not even the west of Scotland, has anything like the multitude of islands one finds in Norway and Sweden.

When we came into the bay the steamer stopped, and I shoved the Rob Roy over her side, stepped in, and in a few seconds I was paddling away on my course, while the Gotha paddled away on hers, and she was soon lost to sight behind a cape. Then I felt happy and free.

It was a supremely fine morning, with a light wind, which died down to complete glassy calm. The silence as I glided under tall cliffs was quite impressive, with rugged rocks above, and strange sea-birds looking down from them. Only now and then there plashed round the headland the break of the long-rolling swell, or the shrill cry of a gull, or the whiffing of the strong wings of the wild goose, sailing aloft in groups of three or five in a wedge-shaped company. Another very large bird, with long, curved neck, also flew past sometimes, and the water had a dark green hue, and the weeds in its depths were new, for it was sea now, and no longer lake.

The first bay we crossed was six miles wide, and then came another of eight miles; and, as the breeze began to freshen here, we stopped on a rock to rest, to lunch, and to set my little lug and tiny jib, and then away again the Rob Roy rode on the waves gaily and fast.[4] For some hours no house was to be seen, and no man or beast; but the feeling of romantic solitude would have been spoiled by these. At length we got among the islands, and then little fishing-boats came in sight, and a cottage here and there, and a white post placed as a mark for ships to guide their course by in this labyrinth of rocks, where it must be fearful work to sail in a winter's night of storm.

Suddenly the wind calmed, and turned about right in my teeth, and a great thick fog-bank came hustling up along the sea yearning to infold the poor Rob Roy in its clammy and dim cloud, like soft cotton-wool. But this happened too late to be dangerous, for we were near enough to shore, though here it was craggy and bleak.

At worst, however, it would only have been necessary to choose a softish rock for the night, and to turn the boat over on it for a roof; and serene sleep may be had even by the sounding wave. This, of course, was only as a last resort; meanwhile I resolved to lie to for an hour, and wait for finer weather; and meanwhile, too, a glass of grog was served all round to the crew, and a double ration to the captain.

The real sea certainly has waves quite different from those even of a large fresh-water lake, however wide its shores. They are more buoyant, without doubt, and they seem to be more dignified. If I *am* to be drowned, let my shroud be salt water.

Moving cautiously among the rocky points, where the fog was so thick that any speed would be dangerous, suddenly a sunbeam split the misty curtain, and I saw a man on the top of a very tall ladder supported in a leaning position. This was a look-out post; and the moment the man saw me, he ran down, shouting as if he was mad, but it turned out to be only an old sailor's joy at seeing so beautiful a boat. Worthy tar! he had been all over the world, as well as "at Newcastle, in Scotland;" he was now, he said, stationed "out of the world." He soon got another boat, and pulled alongside, and then round and round me, with loud exclamations of genuine delight—"So feen, so feen!" so pretty, so pretty! And decidedly the Rob Roy was "mycket bra." This old pilot soon put me on the right track; and I pulled up at the little village of Oxlö Sund,[5] where, as may be supposed, every man, woman, and child came to see the boat, left for half-an-hour on the beach while I reclined on the grass to rest.

This little hamlet is a bathing-place, and the young ladies soon arrived in bevies of alarming strength. The pilot had it all his own way in a lecture about the Rob Roy; and a carpenter measured her every whit, while another wiseacre said she was only a large fiddle.

A steamer was to come past there about midnight, and I resolved to stop until she came, and take my boat on board. This was the second time we had put the canoe on a steamer at night; but it is an anxious piece of work, especially in rain and darkness, and without the steamer coming to the shore. For the rain soon began to patter, and I had to pass weary hours in a very poor inn, away from my boat, and therefore miserable. At last, when the red lantern was run up as a signal for the steamer to stop, some of the men said she would certainly come to the quay to embark me, while others said this particular captain was "not good," and would insist on my going out to him. And so, in fact, he did; therefore, at the last moment I had hurriedly to launch the canoe wholly unaided, tumble my luggage in, and paddle away in the darkness. When we came near him, and the steamer stopped, there were a dozen hands reached down, but all too short to get hold of mine, and just then a great lumbering boat came alongside before I had handed my rope to the steamer, but *after* I had given my paddle to them. It was a moment of great peril to the canoe; and it was impossible not to recollect with a pang that both my coats were on my back (because of the cold), and so if upset there would be no dry things for to-morrow.

The Rob Roy roared a loud shout, but the other clumsy boat would not hear; nor could they see me at all. One foot more, and we shall be plunged under water with a broken bow.

There was nothing for it but instant decision—to shove

off from the steamer; and there was the luckless voyager standing up in a canoe in the dark, and on the waves, and without his paddle, with his long rope dangling in the water !

It is easy enough to stand up if your paddle is retained as a balancing-pole; but the position depicted in the wood-cut was one of no small difficulty. Still, it was best to keep standing, because gradually the wind bore me to the steamer's side again, though I found her side far too well polished for me, as my nails vainly clung to the cold smooth iron.

It may be asked why try to catch this steamer at all? It

was to save me from passing a Sunday away from my reserve luggage, already sent on, with books to read, and other comforts.

The Rob Roy was speedily housed on the steamer's deck, and I tried to sleep in a cabin so close to the engines that it seemed as if all the hammermen at Motala were banging away just under my right ear. At length sleep came when I ought to have been awake; and the end of it was that I was not aroused until the "flicka," or waiting-maid, told me we had arrived in Stockholm. So ended my first paddle on the Baltic.

## END NOTES

1—P.S. — Yes; it has happened even so.
2—On my return this was tried in London, by the appointment of a properly-qualified agent to "look after" the neglected children of our streets, and to send them to their parents, to schools, refuges, or reformatories, or to the police offices, according to their several conditions. This "Boys' Beadle" has been a complete success. The new Education Act adopted the plan, and the writer of this, with four other Members of the London School Board, direct five such officers appointed under the Act.
3—Rapidly the principle has been adopted in England. "Compulsory Education" and "Religious Education" are the two features of the best School Boards.
4—The design on the cover of this book shows the high swell with little wind which fortunately met us in the Baltic. The angle is much exaggerated.
5—Pronounced nearly Oaksely Soont.

# CHAPTER XI.

I OBSERVED but little alteration in Stockholm since my former visit, ten years ago. The pavement is still bad; and the windows always will look ugly when they place the glass level with the outer wall. True, there is good reason for this, because the snow settles in winter on any projecting ledge; but nothing gives a house a more cardbox appearance than this fashion; and, on the other hand, when the windows are deeply recessed, as, for instance, at Taymouth Castle, or Windsor, what depth and solidity and strength, and even comfort, seem to be expressed by this one character!

It is said that the name of this fine capital was given to it when some homeless wanderers, wishing to settle somewhere, put their raft into the current, and agreed to build a town wherever the "stock," or sticks, should rest, which happened to be on one of the beautiful islands now covered with houses.

The Hotel Rydberg is one of the best you can enter anywhere, and cheap as well as good. In the height of the season, and, moreover, in "Exhibition time," you have an excellent room for about three shillings a-day, with those sofas and tables and easy chairs which so many of our

English hotels will not give their guests, although, in most cases, these comforts induce good travellers to come, and to abide.

Among the people you meet in the Sal there are some English, of course, and that party of ladies will keep talking loud enough for us all. "They do stare so here," says one very *bizarre* in her attire: "I really never did see such people to stare at one. Not that I noticed they were staring at me, but Clara saw it." (Oh, naughty Clara!)

Then you adjourn to the reading-room, and with the "Afton blad," or evening paper, duly announcing the arrival of the ship Rob Roy, is the French "Siècle," where we find a Scotchman described under another aspect, as follows:

It seems (according to this French journal) that Scotchmen have different names for things, and they call a leg of mutton after it is once cooked and served up again, by the name of "poor man" (*pauvre homme*), "and one day lately Lord Brightred came to the hotel at Charing Cross, and, being very hungry, asked for something substantial to eat, and desired the waiter to bring him a slice of 'poor man.' The waiter fainted,"—so would Lord Brightred, if he has any conscience in his cannibal mind, when he reads this story.

But then there is the grand broadsheet of the "Times" on one of the little marble tables; and certainly it is a great treat to get the "Times" when you have been absent for a month from solid news. Here is the unwearied giant toiling away even in vacation time; striking straight blows, but above the belt—thundering with sheet lightning that does not kill, but clears the air. While we are idly paddling, he has been searching the close workhouse wards, cleansing the foul cholera pools, exploding the "pernicious nonsense" of doll-dressed parsons, pulling at rich purses for poor far-off parishes, pleading for the maimed, the mad, the wrecked, the blind, the widowed, the hard-up, even for the horses and bullocks, and for the unfortunate bachelor and the timid old maid who are shut up to travel together in a box, where with smoke or without it, both cannot be happy.

We must leave the paper half unread, for we have to see the great Scandinavian Exhibition, opened in Stockholm. This interesting collection of arts and manufactures is not an international one, but solely for the products of Sweden, Norway, Denmark, and Finland.

In some features, of course, there was positive excellence. Look, for instance, at those maps and charts and school-books and literature for the blind; so clear, so practical, and so eminently cheap. On one map you see Europe coloured as to mountains; on another, as to population; on another, as to fertility; on another, as to railway communication; and a child will readily apprehend each of these pieces of instruction presented separately, while even an adult has but a vague idea of what he has seen, when it is entangled with other matters. Then you have a wire-gauze globe, with the stars on it and the earth inside—a most simple mode of beginning with astronomy; and a case of little card-boxes, each holding a few leaves and twigs of various trees, so that botany may be studied even by a ragged-school. The iron-works of Sweden are justly renowned; and here we see them explained and modelled to advantage. The great Dannemora mine we shall explain in our next chapter.

In the Finland and Lapland Annexe are shown all sorts of wild sea-birds and bears and wolves and furry quadrupeds. One great bearskin is so arranged by stripping the skin off the animal's stomach as well as off its back, that it is fifteen feet long—a monster this to be hugged by when your second barrel has missed fire! A series of fearsome pictures are exhibited, rudely drawn on calico in black and red, and very like the on calico in black and red, and very like the grotesque designs of the old Mexican humorists. These are charms used in Finland to frighten away the bears; and very bold must be the bear that is not afraid of these (see fig. 2 in the sketch). There is a man's cap, too, made of a hedgehog's skin, with a hedgehog's face for a peak; and this you may put on if the wild beast only laughs at caricatures. Real art is, however, well represented in the exhibition of modern Scandinavian pictures, among which those by Tidiman rank highest; while the splendid group of "The Grapplers," by Molin, which most of us recollect at the London Exhibition of 1862, shows that sculpture has a fit successor to Thorvaldsen. Then there are the Laplanders' dog-sleighs and their snow-shoes, each being a strip of wood like the letter f, with a strap for the foot in the middle, and the end turned up to glide over the frozen hills. Some of these shoes are twelve feet in length, and that for the right foot is covered at the bottom with a hairy skin, so as to give a hold of the snow in the back stroke for propulsion.

There is the reindeer-sleigh, one trace from the deer's breast and between its legs, and one rein from its head, which the driver flips from side to side as he guides his horned team.

All sorts of boats are modelled here, and you may notice even an "outrigger" rowing-boat, used long ago in Finland (fig. 3, page 112), and called "ekstok"—but coolly appropriated as an English invention on the Thames. High up there hang festoons of gracefully-curved nets, some with fine thread and narrow mesh, to catch the herring and sprat, others with tough rope coils, to wind round the struggling monsters of the deep. Corks are used for some, birch bark serves to buoy up others; but the most improved float seems to be one of glass, blown in an ellipsoid shape, with a knob at each end for attaching it, but no opening. These are of all sizes, from two inches long to eighteen inches. Every kind of fish-hook the most crooked imagination can think of may be inspected here, from the whale harpoon to the little bright silvered hook for herrings, which catches them without bait, for they rush to it merely to have a look.

Among the curiosities brought out by the Exhibition was an enormous whale, which was caught at Göteborg, and has been admirably preserved, and with the mouth open, down which you enter into a neat room, with tables and sofas, and mirrors, and gauze curtains—all inside the great fish. Near to it was the skeleton, with every bone carefully reunited, down even to the rudimental joints of the second flappers, which correspond with the hind legs of other mammalia.

The view of Stockholm from the Mose Backe heights is really the finest view of any town I have ever seen. Water, wood, green fields, white buildings, red roofs, and most picturesque shipping—say where else you can find these so combined. Venice is too flat, Edinburgh wants a river, Pesth is formal, Moscow is dead, and Stockholm must have the palm if my vote is to be given. The picture of all in the eye is fresh with lively bustle, brilliant colour, and graceful form.

In a quiet way the people here can very well enjoy their leisure, too. The island opposite the palace is free to all, even if they do not sip coffee under its trees, or step into the little steamer with its tinkling bell and miniature green and red lamps which will screw them off to the Deer-garden in five minutes for a penny.

In London we have absolutely no place where in September the general public, including Mrs. Bull and her prude daughters, may sit in decent comfort at nine p.m. under a bushy tree, and with gas jets illuminating the fountains and flowers around them, all free. When our town life is contrasted with that of Paris, it is easy to account for our defects: first, by the climate debarring us from evening parties out of doors, and then by our admirable domesticity, which makes all good folks assemble round the family hearth. But these Swedes are as homely as we Britons, and their climate is not more genial; yet one sees even in Finland, still further north, a vast amount of proper enjoyment of out-door leisure which somehow cannot be managed in England at all.

Ladies in England now patronize canoeing, and we have several fair members of our club. Double canoes carry man and wife, brother and sister, and even two cousins (ahem!) Much amusement and healthful pleasure may be had thus in free fresh air on bright merry water. Canoes with four men in each are much used by the Cambridge University branch of the Canoe Club. Their annual race in "scratch fours" of this kind has just come off (March 11, 1872). Instead of the paddle with two blades the single-bladed paddle is best for a double canoe, as there is no splashing, and no "apron" required. For this half-paddle, it will be seen that we go to the Indian and the Honolulu islander, instead of following the Kamtchatkan in his "kyak." The single-bladed paddle, light short, and handy, was used last summer in my Rob Roy on the Zuider Zee,[1] and I hereby strongly recommend it to fair "waterwomen" as the best implement for their propulsion.

Stockholm is the place for a good rest, too, and this was needed by the crew of the Rob Roy; for with all our resolutions to abstain from too violent exercise, we had gradually become accustomed to ten hours a day in the canoe, and this is too much. It is a strain on nerve and muscle. Last year I worked up to that amount only at the end of a three months' tour, and then it brought on a reaction which the strongest frame must expect if overworked. A comfortable hotel, and plenty to see and to do while my boat lies resting on the second floor, at ease, was a wholesome interlude, but it is only a pause, for the sky is fair, and our sails must be set again to the breeze.

END NOTES
1—Published in "Evening Hours" (Hunts'). With woodcuts.

# CHAPTER XII.

Rob Roy in the Press — Ongbots — Lake Mälar — Lake
Hjelmare — Solemn Speed — The Dannemora Mine.

AT Stockholm there was always a large crowd to see the
canoe carried from the hotel to the water; and as we sailed
among the shipping, or paddled up the narrow lanes of
water between the houses, the crowd ran alongside, or in
front, to secure good places in advance.

I once took a fancy at Venice to row a gondola alone;
and with very great difficulty a gondolier was persuaded to
surrender his boat for an hour to my care. Very soon this
novel mode of rowing, in which you stand up and look
forwards, became tolerably pleasant. But when I turned out
of the Grand Canal to some of the lesser creeks I was at once
assailed with screams of abuse from the windows on each
side, and all sorts of missiles were hurled at the gondola.
There was nothing better to be done than to row on and
bear this unexpected attack, which I found was directed
against the unhappy tourist who ventures to work a
gondola without a gondolier. Venice, now risen from the
dust again, and linked to Italy with chains of love and
freedom, must deck her gondolas in bright colours, as of
old, and hire them out to all members of the Canoe Club,
without throwing cabbages at them from the water-palaces.

In Stockholm, however, all was welcome, and smiles
and bows from the fair, and off went the hats of the men as

they shouted from above, "Bravo, Englishman! Good voyage to you." At one place, after returning from a delightful excursion on the sea side of the town, we came to a lock, or "sluice," as they term it, but we landed, hauled the boat over the wall, and went on again steadily as before. This incident was related in the newspapers, and copied again and again, even into papers three hundred miles away.

Winding channels, some as narrow as a garden walk, led me into the country, among high rocks, charming villas, bathing-houses, and orchards, with children playing on the grass, and ladies picnicing under the trees. This, and only this, is the proper way to see Stockholm thoroughly; and we admired it more as we saw more of its beauties. But the air of the place, strange to say, seems by no means healthy, and while our crew was ashore there they had languor all the time.

Stockholm is the very place for a canoe, or any other suitable pleasure-boat ; yet there were few, scarcely any, yachts or rowing-boats to be seen on the water. Not that these would be needed for mere locomotion, because that is admirably provided for by other means; but perhaps, as wealth increases, and men who win enough find the benefit to health which manly exercise affords, we shall hear of more vigorous activity for bone and muscle at play than were observed in Sweden during my voyage.

On the other hand, it is to be remarked that for the more utilitarian purpose of traffic and speedy carriage, the people of Stockholm make far better use of their rivers and lakes than we Londoners do of the Thames.

The water rushes past and round everywhere in rich profusion, clear and deep, and people go almost as much by water as in Venice. The privilege of managing the numerous ferries used to belong to the women from Dalecarlia, a northern province of this long-stretching country. Even after steamers were introduced, I had seen on my former visit some little ferry-boats worked by paddle-wheels turned by

"STOCKHOLM STEAMERS."

these great, strong, healthy-looking ladies, with bright red bodices on their short waists, and heels very high and sharp, exactly in the centre of their shoes (see fig. 5, page 112). But now there is a fleet of lively little screw-boats—the most agile and convenient mode of locomotion one can imagine. Each of these swift, open, "ongbots,"[1] low in the water, and elegantly shaped, bas seats all round the edge; and the ladies' crinolines, as they get in, whisk by the fierce, white glow of the little furnace. The engine is in the middle of the passengers, and one lad manages it, while another sits luxuriously steering. As these steamers are of all sizes, some only as large as a small rowboat, their constant movement, and the puff! puff! of their tiny engines,, creates an animation on the water which relieves Stockholm from being dull—if, indeed, a place can ever be dull which rests upon the graceful eddies of a sunlit sea.

When it was time at last to leave Stockholm, the wind from the west was so strong that I grudged the labour of pulling against it on a lake already traversed before; and therefore put the canoe on a steamer running to Orebro, and stopped the Sunday there. This run of eight hours through the Mälar Lake rather confirmed our opinion that, excepting in the direction towards Upsala, the Mälar is not so picturesque as it is supposed to be. It lacks variety.

A very large school at Orebro attracted my attention, where 500 lads are taught, and after a course of six years they may enter the University at Upsala. They assembled for church on Sunday morning, and many of the townspeople also came. The pupils marched in for the service two and two, the great fellows of twenty walking like the youngest children; and they were seated in long rows, with the gradations of age, or, at any rate, of stature, very strictly observed.

After church about a hundred went to bathe, and they jumped from high ladders and towers into the river, frolicking about for a long time—indeed, far longer than is good for health.

The railway from this place was the first made in Sweden, but it had an inauspicious beginning. The notorious John Sadleir was chairman of the Company, and had won their implicit confidence, until he decamped with £360,000—in fact, all the funds of the enterprise. We were also told that the first engineers sent here from England quite astonished the people by their style of living in a country where their salaries of £500 a year were in strong contrast to the modest stipends of the Swedish engineers, some of whom are not paid more than a tenth of that sum.

We next visited Lake Hjelmare (on September 1st), another great "Sje," too broad to see across, and rather dull on the shores; and then had a long paddle up the Orebro River, and went by rail to Töreboda, the charge for the Rob Roy being *nil*. The canoe had already travelled about 300 miles as a parcel on the railways during this tour, and the expense of all this transit did not exceed three shillings and sixpence.

The Swedish railways are very comfortable in their arrangements, and rather composed in their mode of action—no night trains, no fuss and bustle, even in the day, but a sedate and deliberate steadiness, which is quite a rebuke to our desperate haste in England, where half our energy is consumed in hurrying to a place, as if our lives depended upon doing the journey in so many minutes, and then rushing away from it again as fast as possible.

In Sweden the train stops at least four "minuter" at nearly every station; but it is very punctual in its whole traverse, and you find an excellent dinner, with twenty minutes to spend upon it, about three o'clock in the day. The viands are laid out on a central table, and every man helps himself, and conveys his chosen dainties to some side table, where he can sit down comfortably to enjoy soup, fish, meat, vegetables in profusion, pudding and pastry, coffee, thick cream, and a half bottle of ale, the whole to be paid for by the small sum of eighteen-pence!

There is a deep iron mine in Sweden, very celebrated for its ore, which is said to be the best in the world, and is all brought to England. The Armstrong guns are made from this iron, because it is so tough that it may be rolled into a long strip, and then coiled round a "mandrill" or centre piece, and afterwards hammered so as to unite all the joints into the strong tube of a huge cannon.

The iron must be tough indeed which can stand the tremendous strain of 100lbs. of powder fired inside, with a force that will shoot forth a ball 600lbs. weight, to leap over five miles at a bound. In one of my former visits to Sweden, a Frenchman was travelling with me, when a visit to this mine of Dannemora was proposed, so we hired a carriage and went together; and as it was a curious place to see, perhaps the reader would like to hear about it. We put up first at Upsala, a quiet, dull, overgrown village with a celebrated university, exceedingly ugly too. The *curator* of the museum was a funny old man, with a brown wrinkled face like a walnut, and green spectacles upon his nose. He was very civil to us. He liked to show his curiosities to an Englishman and a Frenchman travelling together. Rain fell in the unlively streets of Upsala, on our return to the inn, and a few people pattered about in wooden clogs, the sound of which echoed drearily along the wet pavement. It was a "stupid place" for the traveller who voyages for excitement, or scenery, or pictures, or music, or fêtes, or bustle; and almost all travellers, especially French ones, must have one or more of these pleasures, or the journey becomes a drowsy task.

But this Frenchman was intelligent and agreeable, so we chatted by the fire together (it was cold outside), and settled to start next morning in the dark, at four o'clock; indeed, he was one of the very few Frenchmen I have met who were travelling for pleasure and improvement, not for business or science. He could not speak English, though he eagerly desired to do so, and when, in the steamers on the Swedish lakes, or along the Gulf of Bothnia, or amid the islands of Finland, he heard Swedish ladies speaking to me in English, and saw them reading our English books, he came near and listened and sighed, because our pleasant talk was all a blank to him.

Next day, then, we rattled along together in the carriage till we came to the mines of Dannemora. The appearance of this place was quite different from that of any iron mine that I have visited. It was something like the slate-quarries near Penrhyn in Wales—a large and open pit, the edges of

which are perfectly vertical, and go down, down, down into the darkness 500 feet below.

The mouth of the pit is seven acres in extent—a terrible vast chasm as you peer over the edge. For three centuries men have been mining there, and the deeper they dig the richer is the ore.

It is a wonderful thing to look into the crater of Vesuvius, and far more wonderful to gaze into the crater of Etna, that smoking bowl a mile and a half round the edge, but to see into this iron mine, where human hands had dug so deep, was a grand sight truly.

If you took St. Paul's Cathedral in London, and set it in this pit, the cross on the top of the dome would still be far below the surface, and yet we could see many men at the bottom, or clinging to ledges at the sides, and hammering away—little pigmies as they seemed—with a faint clinking noise, only to be heard when all was still around, as we lay down flat near the edge, and put our heads over to listen.

The man who showed the place took us to the engine for lowering the workmen into this pit. It was a rude, creaking wheel, worked by two clumsy oxen that turned a wooden drum, and so wound up or let down a very thin iron rope with an open bucket at the end.

After we had gazed for some time into the depth in silence, the man asked, "Would you like to go down?" Each of us looked at the other and smiled. Neither of us wished to go down, but neither of us wished the other to think he was "afraid;" so the jealousy of English and French, and the want of moral courage to say "No!" made us both agree to descend, though nothing new was to be seen below, and indeed nothing was there which could not be seen from above with our telescope.

However, as neither of us dared to draw back, the man hooked the open bucket on the thin iron cord, and the bullocks were harnessed to the crazy wheel, and we stepped into the bucket, and held round each other's waist, for there was scarcely room in the pail for two to stand. Each of us tried to appear composed, and I lighted a cigar, and when the Swede said, "Are you ready?" we were swung up in an instant, and in another moment were hanging free over this awful depth. As the oxen went round, and the iron wire uncoiled (with horrid jerks, too, that seemed as if they surely must snap it), the bucket went gradually down.

The sensation was very peculiar, and quite different from that of going down a coal-pit, or any other mine, where the shaft is only a narrow hole, however deep it may be; for in going down these ordinary mines or coal-pits, you cannot see more than a few yards beneath, so the full depth from the dizzy height is never quite realised by the mind.

But here it was all daylight, and open on every side, and as the bucket dropped down slowly it turned round and round so as to bring all the hideous abyss into full view, and the crags and caves and jutting points of rock, which seemed to move up and come nearer to us as we went down to them. Presently the bucket began to shake, and the iron wire was quivering. Both of us were trembling, too. *He* said it was my fault, but I was sure that *he* was giving way. This, however, was certain, that if either of us became giddy, or faint, or even nervous, so as to lose his hold, one, or most likely both, would instantly have tumbled out of the pail.

Eight minutes—an hour it seemed—having been spent in the descent, we reached the bottom, where the workmen received us with cheers, and then fired several blasts of gunpowder as a salute. We inspected all the operations carried on in this nether region, but I will own that the pleasure of doing this was clogged by the recollection, "We have to get up again."

This feeling spoils much of the delight of visiting a cave, or a difficult or dangerous mine, when you have attained the spot you are to reach, by crawling through some long dark passage with only a few inches or more to spare, and the sensation present all the time "If the rocks shift here in the least, I shall never get out again."

What toil and trouble and danger men will encounter to get at stones that have gold in them!

How little do we labour for the true riches which are "better than gold!"

Our bucket soon began to go up again, and the cheers of the miners sounded fainter as we left them far below. One could not help feeling that if any part of the thin, much worn iron rope, not thicker than one's little finger, were to snap now, there would be instant death! Thus fragile is the thread of life for all of us, and thus uncertain, and yet we plod on, and laugh, and sleep, and sing. How is it possible that any sensible man can live in any sort of contentment unless he has got a better hope of a better life when this short spell is over! Surely it is a mad infatuation which keeps men careless about eternity, and a heartless ingratitude which keeps them cold to the love of Him who died to make us safe for ever.

## END NOTES

1—"Ong" is the Swedish for "steam;" and this word seems quite of a different root from "damp" or "vapeur."

# CHAPTER XIII.

Midnight Music — Catechism — Law and Justice —
Mobbed on the Rail — Good Dog — A Linguist — From
Venern — Sinking Rock.

THE canoe skipper had set his mind upon another pull
on Lake Venern; and they said a steamer might pass along
the canal to the lake that night, so we determined to wait for
this, and meanwhile took a long sail in the West Gotha
Canal. Being without any luggage in the boat, and so near a
dry change if the Rob Roy were overset, I became quite
reckless in sailing hither and thither in the very strong gale
which now commenced and lasted for a week. A great
heavy sloop passed on the canal, towed by two bullocks at
one mile an hour. Another was hauled along by women,
and we noticed a female hodman pulling up mortar by a
long rope to the top of a house.

Night came, so I had to lie down in my clothes, ready
for the warning whistle of any passing steamer, which
would have to be boarded by the Rob Roy in the dark. The
hours passed wearily. When I tried to keep awake sleep
stole upon my eyelids, and strange dreams flitted through
my mind, ending in a start up suddenly for the steamer's
whistle, but it was only the shrill music of the wind. Then
when I tried to sleep wakefulness came on perversely, and
thoughts of home and England coursed through my brain
in rapid march, but linked together only in confusion.

The night was wintry cold, the wind shook the doors, and the rain pelted on the windows gloomily. One solitary light in a neighbouring house had long been a sort of companion to me as I gazed into the dark betimes; at last this too paled down to nothing, and all was blackness. Even my last bit of candle had burned down, and vain was the search for more among many rooms, all with open doors and snoring inmates. Just as it seemed most lonely and all asleep but me, beautiful music came through the wall—the chords of a piano, softly played, and slow. It was the post-master, who rose up to render on the keys some pretty *morceau* he had been dreaming of in bed. The sound of music, and such sweet tones, too, was quite a comfort in this solitary hour; and it was a pleasure to find that the performer is well known for his excellent taste for harmony — that source of universal enjoyment.

The station-masters on the railways are usually retired captains of steamboats—men accustomed to deal with foreigners, and to be prompt and punctual in their times. The guards in the trains are selected from the former stage-coachmen; so that all parties are provided for by the railway, which at first seems to displace them from employment.

Among the numerous visitors to the canoe was a tall, clever, gentlemanly man, who was eagerly curious as to the boat and its journeys. When he saw a tract he laughed outright, and tried to induce the other spectators to join in his ridicule of this mode of presenting religious truth, as likely "to make it vulgar." But laughter is quenched by a solemn tone; and in French, Swedish, and my own native tongue, he was soon brought into a more serious mood. He could not answer the questions, "When is religion 'out of place'? If it is inconsistent with what a man is doing, which ought to give way—the man's actions or the religion? What place do you give religion; and, during last week, how often has it had any place whatever in your conduct or your thoughts?"

For, indeed, it does seem, on reflection, that eternity,

spirit, and the other life ought to have the main field of thought in every breast; and it is for this world, sense, and time to justify their places, as interlopers on the grander themes. Religion is not to be "dragged in" indeed, but is it to be "dragged out" from its rightful place—the throne of the heart?

This being the very first instance in which levity had been shown while I had given about 1000 tracts to rich and poor in this and my former journey, it is a pleasure to mention that it ended well; for the gentleman seemed ashamed, and not only received the little paper, but asked me to write my name upon it, and he wrote his own name underneath.

On another occasion an Englishwoman asked permission to state her case, saying her father had died, and had left her some money by will; but not one penny had she received, and she had applied to the Swedish Courts in vain, "for they would not attend to you unless you had money." She wished me to speak to her English relations to help her, if I "ever happened to meet any of them;" but I at once promised to inquire into the matter on my return, and not to wait until some unlikely chance might bring me in contact with the good lady's relatives.[1]

The gale, which was of unusual violence, and had been telegraphed from Paris as likely to visit the Baltic, probably detained the steamers, for none came past, so we went on by rail to Göteborg, and determined to go by steamer from thence to Lake Venern, to accomplish the resolve as to one more paddle on its broad bosom.

The canoe was as much mobbed in the train as in the water by visitors. At every station there was a crowd about the parcel van to see it; and often a whole train was emptied of passengers, who flocked from their carriages to look at the travelled *kyak*. But in England, too, these boats are novelties; and what think you was the name they were scheduled under, when two canoes came to a Midland station, and the head office was asked how they should be charged? Answer by telegram, "Charge them as invalid chairs—double the price of perambulators." Shade of the paddle end, what an indignity!

The game Captain Dahlander, whom we had met at Carlstadt, had his steamer for this trip; and here was again his faithful, well-remembered, curious old bottle, shaped like a dog, with its glass legs, and the tail for a handle, from whose mouth he had poured a "nip" of brandy, just in time to save me from a chill, and probably from cholera, when embarking, wet and weary, on board his tidy craft some weeks before.

It was a long day of driving rain, but when we reached Venersborg, on the lake, this captain and another, and an Englishman and myself, had supper on shore, and then a curious conversation, in which Captain S— showed his marvellous power of language by speaking even in the same sentence Swedish, French, English, Spanish, Portuguese, Italian, Russian, and even Irish with the purest

" CAPTAIN DAHLANDER'S DOG BRANDY."

Skibbereen brogue. This talented gentleman interested me very much; and a few days afterwards he mentioned that when he had used an oath in our conversation the rebuke of his British passenger went to his heart "like a knife;" that he had next day told his mate of the incident, and was so much ashamed of the oath that he much wished to see me again to apologize. So now when we happily met once more there was room for useful talk; since, however engaging other things may be, there is one great topic of universal interest and of eternal import—the death and resurrection of Christ and His atonement for sin. It was very curious to find a man of deep metaphysical turn and reflective mind labouring in such a sphere, and still more interesting to observe (what we are so prone to forget) that a kind reproof is not without effect, even if at the time it may seem to fall unheeded. He gladly accepted a copy of the "Loss of the Kent East Indiaman," with this inscription, "From the Captain of the Rob Roy to the Captain of the Eos." In return he gave me his portrait.

The great Lake Venern is 143 feet above the sea, and it has more than thirty rivers pouring volumes of water into it, but only one stream issues from the lake to the sea; and so great must be the evaporation from the hundreds of square miles of this inland sea, that this outlet seems to be less in volume than several of the great rivers which flow into the lake. Still, as the deep and angry flood of overflow tumbles down a precipice tinder the railway bridge 100 feet wide, one sees that the great Venern has a good deal of water to spare. After inspecting a tabular record of the fall and rise of the water in this lake since 1819, varying some 16 feet in the extremes, there seemed to be no rule or law discernible as to the relation between the amount of rain falling and the fulness of the water. Probably the other elements that affect this are the wet and dry winds, and the atmospheric conditions which determine the amount of evaporation.

The Gota River rushes out of Venern with a series of mad bounds and vigorous plunges, noisily. The eddies and regurgitations caused by this violent exercise produce some eccentric phenomena, one of which I drove to see, in a pretty wooded glen. This is called the "minute tide," in which a swelling of the water once every minute fills up and empties again a quiet pool a little withdrawn from the river's course. No explanation, it seems, has been given of this periodic wave; but of course there is some regular recurrence of causes which conspire to fill up the pool and then subside, the rise appearing to be about a foot in depth.

Not long after this, when we had paddled into a sequestered bay on this same Goto River, a very curious incident occurred. I had debarked upon a rock islet only a few feet long; and the canoe was lying alongside, as usual, while we rearranged the outfit, provisions, sails, and fishing-tackle.

A strong current gurgled in deep eddies just outside, and a wave now and then playfully lapped my feet. One or two of these waves, having come up higher than usual, I noticed with surprise that the water was evidently rising, and indeed it had nearly covered the little rock, and was floating the canoe.

Immediately the thought occurred that this was another event like the "minute tide," near Venersborg, described above; and we expected to see it soon subside, with no worse consequence than wet feet for our crew. But no, the water rose still, and the isle was covered, and—oh, horrible certainty!—at last it was plain beyond doubt that *the island itself was slowly sinking*. The surprise, fear, and strangeness all commingled in this event it is quite impossible to describe. That a solid rock should steadily go down and leave me in deep water was a thing unthought of, and which no one could be prepared for.

The worst was the *gradual* sinking—had it been immediate, of course I should have only had to swim to the canoe; but the mysterious uncertainty made me lose that decision which danger is always met with by a sort of instinct when you are used to it, and if you have previously contemplated it as at all possible.

Thus, instead of instant action to get away, I kept dancing and turning on the rock—now well out of sight and below water—until at length, with a strange momentary panic, I stepped on the arched deck of the canoe, and positively managed, by some extraordinary balancing manœuvre, to walk along this into the boat from her bows—a feat not to be performed in cold blood, even if you started from the solid ground.

Thoroughly wet, and panting with the intense excitement, and laughing, too, at the extreme oddness of the whole affair, the captain was some time before he could restore order among the ship's company, and things settled down to their regular way.

Meanwhile the current had borne us from the place, so it was not properly investigated; but the inquiring canoeist who seeks the spot is directed to the second bay round the east corner, past the fisherman's hut. Probably the explanation of the occurrence is that a huge rock detached from the shore had rolled into deep water, and happened to be poised on its end, until my weight gradually inclined it outwards, when it toppled over slowly into the darker, deeper depths below.

## END NOTES

1—We much regret to be compelled to remark that the bandage round the eyes of "Justice," when holding the scales in Sweden, is said, on good authority, to admit some rays of golden light.

# CHAPTER XIV.

Bravo! — White Squall — Trolhatta Falls — Urchins —Prisoner — Fishing Sailing — The Whirlpools — Spying — Pretty Sophy — Thanks, Gentlemen!

THE gale and the rain still continued on Lake Venern; but we launched the Rob Roy on the waves amid the plaudits of the spectators and their best wishes for my voyage. The wind was southwest, right in my teeth, and I had a hard pull to breast it; but then the current of water was with me, and when this expanded into Lake Vassbotten the voyage became exceedingly interesting. It was here that in the murky distance I noticed a steamer coming, and steered straight for her, to show to all on board how well the canoe behaved in heavy surf. Just as we neared each other a loud cheer came from behind me. This was from the crowded decks of another steamer, which had overtaken me unperceived because of the deafening sound of the wind; and as now all the passengers and crews of both steamers cheered and waved handkerchiefs, crying, "Bravo, Rob Roy!" it must be owned that the little boat felt a thrill of honest pride in its heart (of oak), and dashed the white spray from its yellow breast with an exuberance of buoyant energy. As for the captain of the canoe, he, of course, was quite impassive under all these compliments; for there are certain feelings, such as pride or vanity or insincerity, which we weak mortals are supposed never to feel, or, at any rate, nobody must ever acknowledge that he is affected by them.

Soon after this a dense black cloud came looming up, and at first so very slowly that it looked all the more unpleasantly mysterious as to what would be the result of our meeting; then a lull came, and it was plain now we were to have one of those terrible white squalls which cover the water with foam whisked from the crest of every wave, and borne along on the blast in a level shower of spray, which instantly blinds your eyes just at the time when the most careful steering is required. To avoid this, I paddled swiftly to land, and pulled up the boat on a low, bleak, lonely islet, where only a cow seemed to live, and a very amazed cow it was. But still there was a sort of shed even here; and in dire

necessity it appeared just possible to find shelter there during the worst of the hurricane. But, alas! this was a very bad move indeed, for the hut was full of water, and ankle deep in mud; and as I clung to the bare wooden planks outside—for it was impossible to get in—I was in constant fear that the wind would carry my canoe bodily away.

The fierce power of these blasts had been already proved in the yard of the hotel where they had turned my boat over, and compelled me actually to hold the canoe down upon the ground with my hands. On this occasion every article I could spare, even my thick shoes, had been left behind me in the reserve luggage, so as to be light for the rapids.

It was this proof of the power of the wind that made me land to avoid this one squall—the only one the Rob Roy ever "shirked"—and now we were in a far worse plight on shore, being quite wet, and covered with mud; though, perhaps, had we faced the storm at this time on the water, the wind might have lifted both me and my canoe fairly off the waves.

The squall passed as quickly as it came, and out burst the genial sun as we floated into the Carl's Graf Canal, and then on the rapid current pleasantly down to Trolhatta, where a good hotel and good dinner and dry clothes soon rubbed away all remembrance of the hard times endured — seasons of exciting interest which arouse the pluck and nerve the muscle of the canoeist, and are the very charms of such a journey as this.

The well-known Trolhatta Falls are certainly worth seeing, as the strong river breaks its great smooth body upon the stronger rocks, and writhes about, dashing up high foam, roaring its loudest and hissing in defiance as its torrent forces a passage to the sea. The navigation of the river is conducted round these cataracts by locks, in a canal lowering you about 120 feet in two hours of tedious work. The passage is curiously cut through the solid rock, and winding here and there, so that it would seem impossible for a steamer ever to get through, but a dozen of them will pass in a day, and not one will even graze the sides, so marvellous is the skill of the Swedish sailors—by far the best for this work that I have ever seen.

Of course it amused them immensely to see the canoe avoid the whole proceeding by my pulling her out on the grass, and running down at a good trot, while the Rob Roy glided smoothly over the green turf, pulled by my hand. A number of boys followed me at a running pace on this occasion; one of them, who helped at a lock, I gave a penny to, and he actually followed for some miles, and caught me at another lock, where another penny made him supremely happy. Another urchin who was carrying one end of the boat happened to slip, and let her bounce on the ground. He ran away at once, afraid and quite ashamed, but a host of ready successors rushed forward to claim the vacant post. They were all much astonished when I gave the first boy twice as much as the new aide, for, poor fellow, he could not help his slip, and he had come twice as far as the other. It is not easy to forget the pleased look of gratitude he gave me for thus reinstating him in his position, and for silencing the gibes of his rivals.

We have heard these little fellows talking for hours about the canoe. "I have seen it," says one; "Seen it," says another, with contempt. "Why, the Englishman gave *me* his sponge to hold;" and then this privileged character becomes at once the centre of information to all the rest. On one occasion a little lad and a man carried the boat through a town; and after it was set down for a moment or so to rest, the man took his place at the front end of the boat, but the boy entreated for his old place, and began to cry, until I found that he wished to be in the front as before—the proud leader of the usual long procession that accompanies the crew on shore.

To cite one more out of many amusing instances of

juvenile curiosity. After the canoe had been safely locked up in an out-house, and hours had passed away, there were still two boys seen at the door, struggling to look through the chinks, one of them lying flat on the ground for that purpose. It seems that a third boy had secreted himself inside the house, to get a better view of the boat; but he now found he was imprisoned there, and a long confabulation of whispers had been carried on with his playmates outside—the point being still unsettled as to whether he ought to beg for release, and bear the punishment of discovery, or remain a prisoner all night.

The weather cleared up as we slowly descended the beautiful Göta, fishing both with the rod and fly and with a long line and trolling hook, sailing all the time; but I do not advise the young paddler to have two lines out at once when he sails down a deep and rapid stream. It is a bit of

aquatic management which taxes all the attention of one who knows his boat perfectly well.

When we came to the upper rapids, which, in a rash moment, we had promised to pass in the boat, there was a crowd ready to see the expected overset; but, after landing for a deliberate survey, I made up my mind that it could well be done. The waves were of the usual character, and there was nothing to fear from these, formidable as they might appear. But there were two unaccountable whirlpools of great size upon the Rhine last year; and the opportunity had been used to practise crossing them until I thoroughly mastered the proper method.

It will be understood that if a boat is loose in a whirlpool, the effect upon it is simply to, turn it rapidly round; and, if the boat is not going at speed, there is nothing more than a little giddiness in the sensation.

But if you are going at full speed down a rapid, and suddenly enter a whirlpool, the water does in reality take hold of the bottom of the boat at one end and forcibly drag it to one side, while the general motion being onward, the result will infallibly be an upset, unless you act wisely. The proper thing to do is to stop the speed of the boat as much as possible, and to lean *inwards* (not outwards, as there is always the desire to do), just as the acrobat in a circus leans towards the centre more and more, the faster the horse he is riding gallops round the ring. The only difficulty in this case was to discern on which side of the boat the outer sweep of the whirl would first catch her, for the course towards this spot was by no means straight, but had to be regulated by the large waves crossing it at the foot of the rapid. We spent about half-an-hour in a very careful examination of all the bearings of this place, though the people were very impatient, and, indeed, some got tired, and went away.

There is also a certain amount of hasty desire to "have done with it" in the mind of a canoeist, when a place of this kind has to be passed; and it is just on such an occasion that deliberate examination is desirable, so this impatience must not be yielded to, or dire may be the result. Probably some neglect of such precautions caused the various upsets which younger members of the Canoe Club had to put up with in more homely places during last summer; and I cannot but suggest that careful examination beforehand is quite as necessary as bold execution when once the actual passage is begun.[1]

Thus the two whirlpools on the Göta were easily passed, and the spectators cheered, as they would have done, no doubt, had she been turned upside down.

In a pretty nook under very thick trees I cooked my last dinner on the rivers of Sweden, and thought pleasantly upon a tour never to be forgotten by me for its interest and pleasant variety. Soon a little steamer passed, and I dashed out to her, and pulled my canoe on her deck. There was a Swedish girl on board, who was reading an English book, and with a dictionary to make out the hard words, so I employed the time in giving her a lesson, gratis, and then drew her portrait; and (to be candid), wrote under it the words "Pretty Sophy."

Next the Rob Roy was put on another steamer, still smaller; and lo! there is on board our amusing linguist, Captain S—, her commodore. The engine of this steamer, however, soon broke down, and after an examination I found it was the air-pump cylinder which had snapped in two. The engineer was a helpless sort of being, but he took advice from the Englishman, for they think, somehow, that all Britons are mechanics; and we wrapped a cloth round the wheezing pump, and so hobbled on till Göteburg was reached again at night.

Next day I made a tour of the pretty town in the canoe, traversing its canals and carrying the boat over obstacles in the streets, until the crowd running after the Rob Roy got breathless in the pursuit.

Before leaving Sweden, it seemed to be a good and proper thing to write a letter to the newspapers, thanking the numerous persons, both, rich and poor, whose hospitality we had enjoyed; and it may be predicted with certainty that if any other member of our Canoe Club brings his boat here, he will have a most kind reception. There cannot be a better wish for him than that he may enjoy as thoroughly as I have done this charming unique journey on the lakes and rivers of Norway and Sweden.

## END NOTES

1—The happy success of the Rob Roy in six voyages — in which she never turned back, and was never turned over — was, no doubt, affected by luck when it was thought to be effected by pluck.

# CHAPTER XV.

Paper Money — Scraps — Mulled Claret — The Volunteers — Swedish National Air — Swedish Soldiers — Over the Sound — Betsy Jane — A Challenge — Copenhagen — Tie to the Dane.

How is it that we Britons cannot keep grave as foreigners do, when a man speaks to them in a ridiculous travesty of their language?

Times and times I must have spoken thus to them; but they never laughed, nor even twitched their lips to keep from laughing at me. Yet, often I had difficulty to restrain at least a smile when a man would enter, hat in hand, as a deputation from visitors outside (the regulation being that at least five must assemble before we could open the canoe exhibition, and lecture for a new audience), "Excuse, sir, we wish boten for see." On one occasion a strange-looking character opened my bedroom door, and putting in his head, he uttered the word "Shavvy?" To which I replied "No shavvy." He was the Court barber; but he knew not that razors were cut dead by the Rob Roy.

Then, again, there was the money of Sweden—the amusing little bank notes, of which a bundle do not come to ten shillings. All sorts of banks rise, flourish, and pour forth a paper stream, and yet nobody examines any one of the notes. None of the banks break—that is good, in sooth; but forgery must be easy and profitable, and, indeed, it is very prevalent, according to the Crime Returns.

Under this head we may observe that the capital punishment applied in Sweden is beheading by the sword; and that when evidence is brought forward short of the direct testimony of two witnesses, the accused is not executed, unless he confesses his guilt, but he may be kept in prison for life. We were informed that in such cases prisoners nearly always do confess, preferring death with a relieved conscience to perpetual confinement. Trials are conducted before three judges, and an appeal lies to three others; but these six are, in fact, a permanent jury, and there is no other.

The post office in Scandinavia does not appear to be well managed at all. Frequently, and during each of my tours, my letters were lost. The electric telegraph we used only once and then a message went forty-four miles in seven hours—rather a mild trotting pace.[1]

No ruins—this is a defect painfully felt in travelling here, just as it is in America. You pine for a roofless abbey or a battered castle; and the woods lack character without a moated grange. Often on the lakes there seemed to be a proud old tower reared against the sky on some distant headland; but when we paddled to it there was no warder keep, and the thing was only rock.

These, you see, are scraps from the stray chips from our log, which must be gathered up before leaving Sweden; and it shows we have come to the end. Heigho!—or Hoity Toity!—whichever of these words is the right thing to say; not that either of them is ever *spoken*.

One more dinner ashore, and so what soup shall we order? Any you please, except that particular hard-named one which came once when we expected a nice hot basin of something, and there was brought in, with all gravity, a plate of cold clear soup with a lump of ice floating in it.

This is worse than mulled claret sent up in a butter-boat, as we had once in Italy, and with a tea-cup for a ladle.

And with our hot soup let us have a glass of white port wine, *i.e.*, the wine of its true colour, not the logwood-port, cooked and painted for John Bull.

The steamer Svea is a most popular boat running from Göteburg to Copenhagen, so she is crammed with passengers, including the crew of the Rob Roy and their boat. After a pleasant passage the steamer is paddling through the Sound, with Denmark on the right hand and Sweden on the left; and the captain yields to my request to lower the canoe there and then into the sea, to the great amazement of all on board.

Away goes the Svea; and the engineer of the Rob Roy receives the command "Ahead easy," while the natives of Helsingborg in Sweden line the shore, amazed to see a canoe approaching them from outside. She was soon housed in the little inn, where she will rest the Sunday, while her crew will go to church in the old brick Minster, not built by Pugin.

And it is on Sunday that, when evening falls, there come the volunteers with their flags and bands; for there has been some rifle-shooting, and the prizemen at least are content. Volunteering has made great progress in Sweden, where the "skarpsjuters" march about and fire for prizes as we do in England. There are 40,000 of them, and they are clothed in a dark-blue uniform, with a neat cap, and black accoutrements. They pay for their arms and uniform, and have from the Government only a small subsidy for prizes and expenses. Their exercise being always on Sundays, I had no opportunity of being present at their drill; but the newspapers continually refer to them, and it is evident that the force is popular, and deserves the interest with which it is regarded.

These volunteers are never tired of playing one particular air, which I had heard also sung by Miss Kjerstin with her tinkling guitar; and so it is printed on the next page from memory, but we think pretty exact. This national

## Swedish National Air.

air, called the "Björneborgarnes Marsch," is a Finland quick step — (played in the Hall of the Dancing bear?)

Here is a translation of it—
BJÖRNEBORGARNES MARCH
*Translated by M. A. G.*
CHILDREN of a race which bled
On Narva's heath, on Poland's sand,
On Leipsic's plains, on Lützen's height;
Still Finland in unconquered strength can shed
Her foeman's blood in crimsoned fields of fight!

Glorious of deed! Our fathers proudly call;
Our swords are sharp, our blood pours free,—
Then forward bravely! battle one and all,
To keep the path of world-old Liberty!

Blest standard! Raise thy faded colours high—
With combats worn, with ancient glories grey—
On! on! and float above triumphantly—
One remnant still of thee will guide our way!

Hence! hence, rest and peace be gone!
A storm is nigh,—it flashes fire,
And cannons roar in thund'ring ire—
In serried ranks press closely on;
Our sires' brave spirits on brave sons look down.

A musical martial Swede thus writes on the subject:—"The march you mention is one that every Swede loves, as it was played by the bands of the Swedish regiments in many a dreadful battle during the unhappy, though glorious war of 1808 and 1809 in Finland—where, in some thirty to forty degrees below zero, the Swedes, half naked and starved, had to fight the Russians as one to ten. That soldiery fought like brave men, but the Government did not back the army, and that was the reason why, when the news came back to Sweden, we quiety deposed our King Gustavus Adophus IV.

"The Swedish volunteers number about 40,000, but are not exactly on the same footing as the English volunteers, as we get no rifles here from the Government, nor any capital grant; the only thing we get here is a kind of adjutant, called "commanding officer," who is generally anofficer of the line at the same time. They shoot very well indeed, but, like the Belgians, never at greater distances than 200 to 250 yards. The officers have not officers' names, as in England, but are called chief of company, chief of subdivision, &c.

"The militia (*beväringen*) is compulsory so far, that every man from the age of twenty-one to the age of forty is bound to go into the ranks to defend his own country; but he can never be taken out of the country. Every man is drilled a fortnight in the spring, at the age of twenty-one and twenty-two—thus a month altogether—at the camp of the regiment of the line of the district, and by their officers. All men from twenty-one to twenty-five are called out first in case of war—and they are some 130,000 to 150,000. They are armed and clad by Government during their two years' drills and in case of war, when they are put in to complete the regiments, so as not to have new troops by themselves.

"I suppose you know how our army is arranged. We have only some 5000 men—guards, marines, engineers, &c.—and some 3000 artillery, who get their pay in money; the remainder are portioned out over the country thus: In every county, or rather (land) lord-lieutenancy, there is a regiment; and peasants and landowners have to grant a house and a certain piece of land ot the soldiers (the landowner, of course, being saved other taxes and *onera* instead), which piece of land the soldier uses for himself; the landowner being bound, in case of war, and durin gthe annual camps, to take care of his harvest, &c. Then each regiment meets at a camp every year for about three weeks' drill.

"The officers of the cavalry and line are paid in the same manner; they have a certain sum of money, and then a house and piece of land, according to their rank, given (and the house kept in condition) by the Government.

"For all that, the Swedish soldier—who gets a pension when he gets old in the service—is very well drilled indeed—much better than the French army; and, as the officers always must live within their regiment, they are known and beloved by their men, who would willingly go into fire and death for them. There is not an instance in history of a Swedish regiment having left their officers. This arrangement was made by Charles the Eleventh in the latter half of the seventeenth century—somewhere about 1680, I believe."

Helsingborg is, no doubt, a very old town, for surely the entrance to the Baltic must always have been an important place for ships, and also for men; and now that Russia claims the Sound as an *appanage* in the dowry of the Princess Dagmar, this ancient strait is more than ever interesting. This is the day we are to cross over it from Sweden to Denmark. It *sounds* grand as a feat to do, but the passage is at most only three or four miles; and in a gloriously fine morning the canoe was carried down to the water, and my paddle plashed in the new ripples, eager for the start as a horse paws for a gallop.

Sun and a fresh breeze, but not too much of either. A long and regular rolling swell seemed to tell that the sea would only calm down in a dignified way after its rage for a week. Ocean was at last in good-humour; but, nevertheless, he was not to be trifled with, so we skimmed over his face daintily, lest the sleeping sea might be awaked. Soon the old grey towers of the Kronberg, on the Danish side, showed clearer and looked almost lively under the morning rays, while the spray spurted up somewhat lazily against its sea-worn walls, now hoary with the splashes of many centuries.

Ships in a long procession moved towards the Baltic,

with the sun on their sails, but there was no flapping of canvas, nor sense of hurry or pressure; neither weary, dead calm nor sudden blasts, but a gentle, graceful bowing of majestic forms, and the canoe itself seemed to relish the fine, long swell. Who that has loved his boat well but does not impersonate her? Reason as I will, there are moments when I think that the Rob Roy is vertebrate.

The sight was too fine to hurry past it, and as we had run across so quickly we dawdled now by the shore; and I paddled out to a bark with British colours flying, and her pretty white sails scarcely full. "It may be some romantic ship," thought we, "and bound on some heroic cruise;" but when we came alongside, it was only the "Betsy Jane, from Hartlepool," with a cargo of coals for Cronstadt. The pure sea water was so clear, and the sun shone down into it so far, that I could see well under her great firm keel, and there was a sheen of yellow light from the copper of her big round waist far below and wondrously supported on this transparent water, making me feel, too, what great depths were beneath me, and how very thin a plank was between.

One great advantage of touring in these temperate parts is this: that the sun is looked on as a friend. When he gleams over the sea in the morning, it is pleasant to feel he will be hotter every hour till noon; whereas, in the sunny south, you learn only to fear the great blazing orb, and every hour of his shining brings it nearer to the time when you have to leave him to rule alone, and the fierce glory drives you into the shade until evening. Idlers we had left on the pier in Sweden, and we passed idlers more on the Danish pier, who had, of course, seen the little boat gliding over the waves, and welcomed her arrival eagerly. Here they mistook me (as in other places) for the adventurous Yankee, "Red, White, and Blue," though my voyage is not of that fashion—artificial hazard without pleasure, and in a purposely difficult and tedious way—two lives sure to go if either man gets ill.

If any one can devise a better method for going over land and water than the canoe, we will gladly adopt it.

The Rob Roy was next carried into the town, and the grave officers of the custom-house were laughed out of countenance as usual when the boat was paraded for formal examination at their street door, so we took her right up to the pretty house of the British consul, whose brother had visited this place with me in 1855. It was very pleasant to be welcomed in a new country, and at a well-covered breakfast-table, and then to luxuriate amongst the currant-bushes, and play croquet with the young ladies, while the boat reposed in the coach-house, where visitors soon came to see her admirable shape. In an album here my kind friends had preserved a little sketch I had made, eleven years before, of a pretty boy standing, hoop in hand, beside the tomb of Hamlet. The boy in petticoats is now a bold Guardsman; and Hamlet, we know, was not from Seland, but from Jutland, his name being Amlet (madman). Then the Cockney says it right, after all.

The croquet had gone on until Rob Roy became a "rover," so she was next embarked on a steamer, and when well on its course, I lowered the canoe into the sea, and spent the rest of the day coasting along the pretty shores of Seland, until countless villas, pleasure-boats, and bathing-boxes announced that Copenhagen was being neared. Stately ships sailed alongside me in gallant array, while carriages and pedestrians were on the road quite near. It was like a lively, bustling street, with the ships for carriages, and the land traffic on the pavement.

The Rob Roy, carried through Copenhagen, of course attracted a great crowd, and the head waiter (being a man of sense) conducted her upstairs, where the great ball-room was allotted for a boat-house, and there the canoe rested gently on an ottoman. We had seen the great sights of this very interesting city long ago—and is it not often a great relief to be able to say this?—but our interest in Denmark had been much increased by perusing a book called "Denmark and her Missions," by Mrs. Ellis, which recites the remarkable activity in early times of the Christian people of this fine old Protestant country. Denmark has done much for English Christians when our own blind policy prevented Englishmen from giving to India the Book which has been blessed to us—the Holy Bible.[2] These times have, happily, changed, but our debt of gratitude still stands to Denmark; and now we are united to the sturdy Danes by the tender tie of a Royal alliance.

Pious and gentle in her wifely care at a bedside watched in deep gloom by all who felt for England's trial. Smiling in bright thankfulness when all of us gave thanks under that great dome one day.

God bless the Danish Princess—our English Queen to be!

## END NOTES

1—The grand news of the telegraph-cable being laid between England and America reached me on a wild lake in Sweden. News by the former cable had reached me in a wild forest of New Brunswick. May peace throb through the wire instantly and for ever!

2—Some information on this subject from the work here cited will be found in the Appendix.

(Editor's Note) Princess Alexandra of Denmark was to marry Victoria's eldest son Albert Edward, but he caught typhoid and died on Dec. 14, 1861 at the age of 42. Her daughter, Alice, married Prince Louis of Hesse. In 1863, her second son, now the eldest, whom the family called "Bertie," was officially created the Prince of Wales and married Princess Alexandra of Denmark. Subsequently, Victoria supported Prussia (of which Hesse was part) during its war with Denmark over the Schleswig-Holstein region, even though her daughter-in-law, her ministers, and her people supported Denmark.

# CHAPTER XVI.

Big Buttons — Canoe for the Casual — Beds! — Rob Roy
Senior — An Old Friend — Inquisitive — Sprogé Island —
The Great Belt — Lost a Head — Down, Down — The False
Stroke — Lake Dull — Green Sailors — Polite in Peril.

THREE Russian frigates in the harbour attracted much
attention. On board one was the youthful Grand
Duke—who is a sailor prince; and one of his preceptors—an
Englishman—was at the hotel. The big guns of the Rusky
ironclad were booming out a salute for the Emperor's name-
day, and the carriages of the King of Denmark, with
servants in red liveries, were bearing guests to the royal
dinner for the occasion.

But I went to the prosaic business of buying an oilskin
coat—one of those bright yellow garments you see on
regular sailors in a regular storm. That which I chose had
double thickness in the back and epaulets on the shoulders,
and most appalling black buttons down the front—all for
the trifling sum of 6s. 6d. It will be understood, we hope,
why this event is narrated in our log. So important an
addition to the stores of the Rob Roy cannot be passed over
in silence, as if one were on a mere common tour, where the
traveller does not carry his own goods over sea and land,
and where another garment added to his luggage is a very
small affair.[1]

In approaching the harbour of Copenhagen we had

descried a man in a canoe (as it appeared) with a long double paddle; and, of course, a rival in the art could not be passed without examination. Next day I went and had an hour's exercise in this strange craft, which was for hire at the bathing- place, with several others. It is a double canoe, with a common chair fixed upon the two hulls, so that you seem to sit upon the water, and then, with a very long paddle—the handle hopelessly heavy, and the blades uselessly small—you can move about in a mysterious but unsatisfactory way upon the quiet waters of the sea. We have noticed these articles frequently on the Continent, and it is rather strange that we have so very few of them in England.

The landlord of the comfortable hotel, quite a gentleman in manners, and warmly attached to England, invited me to supper in his apartments, underneath the great building, where the fame of the boat brought visitors to see it and the sketches, and it was arranged to take a photograph of the

Rob Roy next morning. Meantime, while we lounge and gossip, a young lady comes in for her nocturnal practice on the piano, and has half-an-hour "at scales" with commendable exactness. The cricket club began their season today, but they are young hands as yet.

Having walked and talked, paddled and sailed, eaten and read and written and sketched as usual, I must now go up to prison—I mean to bed. Yes, I *will* have one fling at those detestable Continental beds, and be done with it. Horrid cribs, boxes made for people five feet high; you cannot have a stretch in one of them. Each night I begin with a vigorous push, and the end boards of the structure creak again, trying to make sixty-six inches into six feet six. Laugh not at this grievance as a small one; only he knows its plague who has paddled all day, and wants at length to lie. Ye Swedes and Danes who read this page, have mercy, I beseech you, on tall Englishmen!

The Russian sailors perambulated the town, clad in blue jackets and white cloth caps. One of them made a great noise as he was captured by the guard, and taken away drunk to his ship, where no doubt, poor fellow, he would have a hard penalty in that rigorous service.[2]

The canoe was now put into a cart, and trotted off to the railway which crosses Seland, and here a young German came up, and said he had been with Mr. Lawton in his yacht Sappho on the coast of Norway, and had seen the old original Rob Roy, lent by me to that gentleman for his trip to the North Cape, also that paddle-wheels had been tried upon the other canoe, the Rollo, but they were found to fail (for the five hundred and fifty-fifth time). It was truly agreeable to hear of the good health of the brave old boat; and she is now turned out into a paddock for the rest of her life, though I must say the new Rob Roy is an immense improvement on her predecessor.

At the refreshment-station a man is making a horrid row, and disturbs all the passengers. The face and voice of

the rioter are familiar. Yes, it is my English room-companion
of the Norway inn, who, it may be remembered, walks and
talks in his sleep, and persists that he is not mad. But let us
flee back to our carriage, where also there is a German from
Valparaiso, who says that the Chincha Islands, from whence
comes guano for the farming world, may last, as a supply,
for ten or twelve years. The first cargo of this valuable
manure was imported by a Frenchman. People then thought
he was demented, and they refused to charter a ship for
such a purpose. But millions are now made out of the trade,
and most of this by an English house. At the other side of
the island of Seland, the Rob Roy was marched into the
"Hotel Store Belt," to the utter amazement of the waiters;
and yet they soon gave her a room to herself, for I have now
got bolder in my requests on this point, finding it a very
convenient arrangement to take my cedar companion
upstairs at once.

The plan looked successful here also, especially as the
porter gave me the key of the room. But next day I found
they had retained another key, and scores of people had
been admitted to the nautical exhibition, and had deranged
the fittings of the boat, vainly striving to put them back as
they were before, and to escape the detection sure to follow
when the sailor's knot I always tie round the paddle has
been at all disturbed.

It is to be remarked that the Swedish, and even more the
Danes, are far worse in their obstinate inquisitiveness about
this boat than the Germans were last summer. It had now
become a positive difficulty to keep the canoe still one
single hour, its proper rest was seriously disturbed, except
in my own bedroom; but the whole transaction, let us
acknowledge, is out of the usual line; and when I am
dusting the canoe on two chairs, with its varnished cedar
deck resting on my knee, in a room upstairs, it is difficult to
believe that, in five minutes, this slender airy little thing will
be lowered into the waves, and will buoyantly dash over the

sea, carrying me where many of the roughest sea boats would not be safe for a moment. The wind had again risen so high, and it was so completely unfavourable, that we could only look at the island of Sprogé, six miles away there, among the white-tipped billows, dead to windward, and thus quite beyond my power to visit then; but it was the only occasion on which I had to forego an intended excursion. This little rock lies half-way across the Great Belt; and when the sea is frozen here in winter, people are sometimes detained a week before the ice is strong enough to bear, or has cleared away to let the water be used for sailing. The passengers, however, cross in ice boats, made with three keels and flat bottoms, so as to slide on the ice, or float in the water.

The waves in the harbour of Körsör were high, as the west wind blew against the stream rushing from an inland salt lake; and a dismasted vessel in the offing, and the treble-reefed sails of the few inside, showed there was a stiff gale blowing. However, I launched the Rob Roy fearlessly, and had a charming time of it (quite wet, of course, with spray), bounding over the rollers and dashing through the white water, while the whole population assembled on the pier, and all the hotel, railway, and steamboat people, longing to see how the bar would be crossed by the little "kyak," as they call it—the Greenland name, and which, oddly enough, is very like that of "caique," the name of the Turkish boats on the Bosphorus.[3]

The strong current ran one way, and the strong breeze blew the other; so that the canoe, being about equally affected by these forces, could in fact easily be propelled in any direction, and its manœuvres probably looked wonderful to those who were not aware of this fortunate compensation of forces.

But their plaudits gradually urged me to more daring trials; and at last, having got out further than usual, and among the waves sharpened by the wind and tide opposing, I lost my head once and for a moment—and for the only time in this or the former tour. So the manner of it shall be explained.

When waves are long enough to allow the boat to descend the face of one, and then to rise on the back of another without being caught in the trough between them, then it is really of no consequence how high they may be, for the canoe will ride over each wave like a cork. Now it will be found that, unless you are going fast through the water, about twenty feet between the wave crests will just allow of this regular mounting and descent; but a less distance requires special management.

On this occasion I had got into a position where it was not expedient to turn the boat round, and so we were therefore returning stern foremost—which practice enables one to do quite safely—casting a glance over the shoulder at each stroke, to see the nature of the next wave which has to be encountered.

The Rob Roy was progressing gallantly thus, going with the wind and against the tide. In such cases your motion is always faster just at the summit of a wave, where the wind is strongest; and as the great splash comes at that moment, you cannot see more than one wave at a time, so as to profit by the glance, especially if you are paddling backwards.

On arriving at the top of one of these billows, I suddenly saw that the next one was quite thin (the light shone through it), and the top was curled over. The proper method of "taking" this (according to the excellent instructions of the Life-boat Institution pamphlet) is to rush at it, so that you may have "way" on, and the wave may not drive the lower end of your boat under water, and then turn her over on this as a pivot.

But, forgetting at the moment that I was at this time going stern foremost, which, of course, reversed every operation, I gave a powerful stroke precisely in the wrong direction, that is to say, *forwards*, and thus both my own arm

"THE FALSE STROKE."

and the high-topped crest drove the bows of the canoe deep into the base of the wave before me.

As the cedar deck disappeared foot by foot (but all in an instant of time), it flashed upon me that I had made a fatal error; the likely consequences were too well known. My nerves shrank up as when a schoolboy expects the cane on his hand; and the man at the helm fairly lost his presence of mind. Down came the great curved crest full on my back, and deluged me with water, which easily rushed in round my waist, for the apron is not so secured in the rear as to stand an attack from that quarter.

A good ducking was endured, and a good lesson was learned, "Never go stern foremost against short seas;" and for the benefit of brother paddlers this incident is related at length, while other readers will please to excuse the long story, and to congratulate the Rob Roy on escaping great danger by the buoyancy derived from its high-arched deck.

As it was impossible to reach Sprogé, we. had to turn from the Great Belt into a large expanse of salt water behind Körsör, like an inland lake, which we determined to explore. It is, I do believe, the very dullest lake ever seen. Flat, straight, and bleak sides, with few trees, and scarcely an island. But then the water was clear, and it was very amusing to watch the crabs and fish below. One crab when disturbed actually ran off with its little baby under its arm. Directing my course to the only house, I stole up to it through reeds and shallows unperceived, and began to sing a doleful air under its windows, quite close to the door, for there is no tide here, and so they build within a foot of the water.

Amazement filled the habitation at once. The first boy who came out screamed loudly to the inmates; and, like a wise boy, he kept steadily looking at me all the time he roared. In general they run away to call their friends, and then on their return the sight has vanished, though I often delay in such cases, that the poor fellows may not be disappointed.

In the distance we noticed a sailing-boat labouring very much, and evidently directed by very indifferent seamen; so we bore down to her just as she managed to take in sail, and not a moment too soon, before one of those terrible squalls which sweep over sea and land here with great and sudden violence. One man in the boat had a black frock-coat on and a black "chimney-pot" hat; and this convinced me that the craft needed help, for no one accustomed to boating would keep on such head-gear in a sailing-boat when it blows hard. We found the two adventurers had come out purposely to see the "kyak," and they had been blown away to leeward until they were hopelessly out of reach of home. The ballast in the boat was partly of loose bricks—about the most dangerous things one could carry, as they roll and tumble over in a lurch, and would always fall to the wrong side, just where they are not wanted.

The other navigator was a young lad, who was labouring with all his might at an oar, but still was so polite that he did not forget to take off his hat to salute me even under these desperate conditions. However, with a little assistance and advice, we soon got things to rights; and one must hope that the two inquisitive sightseers will not go to sea again in this plight—at least until another kyak visits the neighbourhood.

And then, after four hours of healthful exercise, returning to the "Great Belt Hotel," how much you relish a cup of coffee! that good coffee which you get on the Continent almost everywhere, because they roast it fresh every day, and grind it not, and put plenty in the pot; and which you seldom can get in England, because we insist on buying it roasted and ground, and, therefore, as it were, dead, and then put little in.

## END NOTES

1—Our Danish dreadnought had some hard times after this, as narrated in The Voyage Alone in the Yawl, Rob Roy.

2—At the Piræus, in Greece, we once went out to the Russian fleet in a little sailing-boat, and then observed in the men-of-war's boats the coxswain lash the men who were rowing with a very long coach-whip. Probably he did not know that an Englishman was looking on.

3—The "Verangian Guard" mentioned in history as a Swedish contingent in Constantinople 500 years ago may have come from the Vrangs River, and have given the name kyak to the Turks.

# CHAPTER XVII.

Girls don't matter — Stolen — Attack on the Forts —
Sönderburg — Libels — Forts of Düppel — Soldiers' Graves.

NEXT morning we embarked in the Diana, a fine
steamer, which makes a cruise among the islands; and here
the Scotch engineer, with his "steeple engines from" Mr.
MacNab's in Glasgy," was glad to welcome a compatriot,
and to receive a "British Workman" for his daughters. The
scenery on this voyage was very pretty, but never grand.
Fine rocks, luxuriant foliage, sparkling sea, and comfortable
houses—all in endless variety of combination and outline,
and with a brisk gale to heighten the interest, while the fine
vessel pitched and rolled delightfully. Crossing from Seland
to Funen or Fyen (pronounced almost Fuin), our course was
then round the southern end, and up a long strait to
Svendborg. This picturesque town captivated my attention;
but when we thought of "how can we get away again if we
stop here to-day"—perhaps it may be for three days — the
idea of stopping at all had to be given up. Long warps had
to be led round the bulwarks of the steamer to turn her
round in the narrow inlet; and this operation was not an
easy one, even with four stout hawsers, for the west wind
now had a strong hold upon us. A youth who could speak
French told me I was the only passenger for Sönderburg
except two peasant girls, and it was doubtful whether—the
sea being so high—we could venture to touch there, and it

would make three hours' delay. I was sorry for this, because we had desired to go there to see the battlefield of the Slesvig campaign; but when my friend said, "As for the girls it is no matter," we saw he meant only his own convenience, and to me it seemed right to think of the poor women, too, for whom it might be very important not to be carried away. Then they said the Prussians would not let me land without a passport, &c., &c.; but all this made one more anxious for the adventure.

There were several Slesvigers and Holsteiners on board the Diana, and they had a very lively conversation in their peculiar lingo, as the island of Als came nearer in sight. They looked on the fine bold cliffs, the waving trees and the deep green grass and thriving homesteads of their own land, occupied by the Prussians, as you would look at your gold watch in a thief's hand—a watch that had been yours for years and years. For there was the Düppel windmill, and the forts all round, sloping wedges, like disjointed pieces of railway embankments, and covered with grass. Sentries were thickly posted on every height, and lounged near their sentry-boxes, striped black and white—the Prussian colours—and with their needle-guns nearly horizontal on their shoulders. In 1864 this bay was the battle scene, and the big guns sent their balls across it, three miles, over the water. Only the day before we arrived the Prussian fleet had visited the place, and now it was empty, except that some herring-boats scudded homewards, with their square high sterns pierced with little windows, exactly as one sees in pictures of a hundred years ago.

Turning now into a narrow channel, we come to Sönderburg; but our steamer rolls deeply in the waves, and must not venture to the pier, so there is nothing for it but to drop the canoe into the sea, and go ashore in her—the offer of going in a boat with the canoe towed behind being respectfully declined by the Rob Roy with as much courtesy as her sense of the indignity would allow.

A canoe, and such a mode of landing, were, no doubt, quite novel at this place, and the beach was soon thronged with visitors, all holding their head-gear on in the high wind, and with their coat-tails flapping in the breeze.

However, I did not mean to come ashore for several hours yet, but only to land my black bag, and then to take a cruise for the rest of the afternoon, and to debark quietly when the excitement had subsided. But the watchful guards were far too sharp for that.

All the soldiers off duty, and with their white canvas jackets and neat round peakless caps, at once rushed down to the canoe; and the authorities solemnly proclaimed that the Captain of the strange craft "must go to the Prussian Custom house," to pay for the Rob Roy. "Nonsense," I said, "I am going to paddle up the bay." "Well, but you must bring the boat to the Douane." "Very good; after my cruise." "No, at once; now." "Please tell them I travelled in Prussia and never paid anything." At last the Inspector, seeing I was English, and that my Monitor was not ironclad, allowed me to go in peace, and the population rejoiced, for they followed along the shore while I led the way in the water. So we had a fine day's exercise and a thorough exploration of the neighbourhood after all.

Sönderburg is a very pretty place, far too lovely for a bloody battle field, and battered houses and trees scarred with shot, and mangled corpses on the ground. The Prussian garrison of 1600 men fill that large square building by the water's edge, and sentries are all round us, while every hill has its forts, and newly-patched houses show where the cannon told on the hapless town. The town is a thriving one, and the people seem very merry under their invasion; indeed, there is more of whistling and singing here than we have remarked for the last two months.

The little "Als Sund" inn was close to the water, and, therefore, good for me, though it had naturally the usual features. First, the box bed, with sloping pillow and footboard, far too short; but we have settled an account elsewhere with this Scandinavian couch, so let it be. Then there is the saucer of a basin, and teacup of a water-jug, and handkerchief of a towel, and the blind that won't pull down or stop up, and the pepper-box that won't pepper, and the door that won't lock, and the bell that won't ring, and, finally, the maidservant that won't go away out of your room—nay, bolts in to see you at any hour—all hours, night or day—and without the slightest attempt at a knock beforehand. Pooh! these are the trifles of travel; and it is really too bad even to allude to them when so many days of glorious pleasure have been enjoyed with zest by the crew of the Rob Roy.

But we mention these things now because they are, in fact, more troublesome than any of the peculiar inconveniences appertaining to this special mode of touring in a canoe. For instance, somebody has lightly said that, "it may be doubtful how far one could enjoy a voyage with one's legs cramped in a boat, and water trickling down both sleeves." To this we reply that it is very little doubtful that a walking tour would not be enjoyed if you had your feet cramped in your shoes—only, knowing this, you get shoes to fit your feet, and so they are not cramped. Why, the canoe must be made to fit the paddler, too, and then there is no cramping at all.

As for the water in your sleeve, it is far better there than down the nape of your neck or about your knees, which we must all put up with in a pedestrian tour. The man who shrinks from water, indeed, had better not go to sea; and the man who sneezes at dust should keep off the dry road. For myself, I like water even at my elbows; and a dash of the salt spray from a glittering wave is not the worst thing you can have in your face. Pardon this logic of enthusiasm—for it is a skipper defending his craft.

It was very interesting indeed to walk round the fortifications, which extend for miles about the town, and

are all kept in apple-pie order, with smooth green grassy slopes, and sentry-boxes, near which you see the dapper Prussian sentry pacing about on a ploughed field, and near him the milkmaid stoops beside the unreluctant cow, and the miller goes aloft to furl the sails for the night.

In my lonely walk through the pleasant fields there were often seen those little wooden crosses set up by some hedge to show where a soldier fell, and on the top of this hill is the cemetery of the battle, where Danes and Prussians are buried side by side.

Here is a Prussian grave—a stone obelisk with a railing round it, and immortelles hanging in the wind, while the inscription reads : "Hier ruhen 25 tapfere Preussen," and near it one of the Danish tombs—a huge stone block with only one side polished, and not so likely to be carried off for a doorstep, or to face the corner of a bastion, as a squared edge stone would be. There are no wreaths about it, but in golden letters, which glitter in the sun, it tells us, "Hier ruhen 209 tapfere Danen. Sie fielen am 18 April, 1864." In many other places were those signs of battle-days which last so long in an unmistakable green colour of the grass; and I recollect having noticed this very distinctly on the field of Culloden in 1845, just one hundred years after the bloody battle there.

The soldiers all look intelligent, healthy, strong, and active young fellows, much like the *matériel* of our best volunteer corps; but their artillery and mortar practice, at least when we were present, appeared to be slovenly and bad. They have certainly improved *that* a good deal before they battered Strasburg and Metz.

# CHAPTER XVIII.

England Abroad — Invaders — Pickled Tongue —
Explosion — Wrecked — Drift on the Reef — Crying for
Joy — Saved.

AT night some people, carousing late in the inn, were
very noisy in the room next to mine, and only separated by
a thin partition; so, when at eleven o'clock they had sung a
most lugubrious song over and over, and worse each time, I
gave two loud thumps on the door. Instant silence, and then
a jabber of consultation as to who and what was this.
Finally they concluded it was "the Englishman with the
kyak;" and then, though the most inveterate of them still
hummed a little, as a sort of assertion of their rights, the
heart of the harmony was dried up, and it soon withered
away into quiet. Certainly it must be highly
uncomplimentary to hear a great knock on the door in the
finest part of your best song. Remonstrance by words could
be answered, but the decision of a loud smack on
resounding wood, though not an articulate message, is
without appeal, and admits of no argument. Sorry as I am
to limit any one's pleasure for my own comfort, it must be
confessed that the Rob Roy would go very slow and very
short journeys if her sailing-master had not plenty of rest as
well as plenty of work.

At a book-shop we had found Harrison Ainsworth's
"James II.," and we read it with very great pleasure. The
strange sensation of reading a thoroughly English book in a

foreign land cannot be described, but it is very powerful. Just as one gets fully engaged about Whitehall Palace and the Earl of Sunderland and the trial of the six bishops and Westminster Hall, and when the mind and body are in the frame as if one were in the very heart of London—out brays the trumpet of the Prussian garrison, and the roll of the drum rattles the "tattoo" in quite a foreign accent, and all one's ideas are shaken and disjointed for a moment, till the mind separates the two facts that one is reading of old England, but in the island of Als. Something of the same kind I had felt in the desert of the Atlas, where one day I kept on reading "Adam Bede" in a cave so long that the Kabyle guide fell fast asleep, and the sun had gone down too far for us to proceed to our halt-place for the night.

On Sunday the soldiers went early to church, and they came back, not in military order, but in groups as they pleased; but there was a quietness and manly courtesy about these men which was very attractive, and we could not help admiring their whole appearance, though, of course, in this country they are looked on as invaders, and England is not praised for allowing the deeds that were done. I do not know the very right in this business; but on the whole, as a general conclusion, we may be glad that a Protestant Constitutional power is consolidated in Europe.

As a tourist, and coming from a land where foreign occupation of our homes is even unimaginable—and, with our volunteers to avert it, we may say quite impossible—there is extreme interest felt in watching the behaviour of the invaders and that of the subjugated people. How must it be to see every day the graves of the men who fought on our side, and were beaten—so fresh, too—and of brothers and fathers. Surely the mourner's tear must sometimes have been dried on his cheek, by the burning heat of revenge, and with clenched teeth.

Next morning I was quite unresolved what to do, and in such cases it is best to go out and lounge about a little, to see if anything will "turn up." In this state of things an English-speaking captain came, and after he had seen my boat (it is good policy always to interest them first) I asked him to help me to get a cart to take the canoe four miles overland to another arm of the sea. He said he had a cart in his ship; so we went to see the vehicle, but it turned out to be a *"chart."* We ought to have used the word "waggon."

If a foreigner talks wholly in one tongue, either foreign or English, it is much easier to understand him than if he mixes the words of both; for in this latter case you are perplexed as to which language you must refer a particular word to. Thus, on another occasion, I was completely puzzled when a waiter inquired if I would have "fleisch eller am?" and I kept repeating the word, "Am! am!" searching the small lexicon in my mind as to what that could be. After all, it was only our own British "ham" he meant.

But here comes a little steamer to the quay. "Where is your steamer going?" "Flensborg." "Will you take me and my boat?" "Yes, we will wait five minutes for you." In half that time my plan was changed and my bill paid, and the boat being hoisted on the steamer, we put to sea. This little Apenrade was the smallest sea-steamer I ever saw, with an engine of 12 horsepower, and after we had gone well out into the swell she pitched most vigorously. There happened to be two other ship captains on board, one of them an old hand from California, and both could speak English. Then there were also the captain of the Rob Roy, and a lady and two children, and a few nondescript "bodies." While I was congratulating myself on the lucky chance of getting a lift to my next destination, suddenly a loud explosion took place, bang! bang! and then a crash and the smashing of glass and hissing of steam and shrieks from the lady, and then utter silence—the engine had stopped. At the alarm, the engineer rushed to the engine; but the stoker, a coward, ran to the bows, to drop into the water. We found the cylinder was blown to pieces, and, of course, the steam-engine was now useless. Here, then, were we, miles from land, and in a stormy sea, with heavy weather to windward, without masts, sails, oars, or even a boat—indeed, they had not even bread on board. The captain took it all in a careless way, as befitted one who could put to sea thus unprovided; and he laughed in a vacant manner, rather undecided what to do. However, we soon made him stir his wits. We hoisted a flagstaff for a mast, and made a great lug-sail out of the black tarpaulin from the luggage, with a boat-hook for a yard. This was done to bring the steamer round before the wind, for she was now lying like a log in the trough of every swell, and we wished to get her into the track of other vessels, whence help might come before the Apenrade drifted to the rocks on our lee. The oldest captain was told off to hold the halyard of our jet-black sail, and he had to lean forward with every swell, so as to ease the crazy mast, in a very comical manner. Soon the weak little stick broke, but not entirely, and I helped, by using another pole as an oar, and rowing with all my might, to get the little steamer round. Then I advised that we should hoist a signal of distress, and all stand up on the bows, and open our coats to act as a sail. This was done, and at length we slowly veered round, and began to run for shore before the wind.

The chief danger was, first, that if night came on before we were seen, there was no food, except three bottles of ale, for about fifteen persons, and no boat to get it by but the canoe; and, second, that we were drifting on to a reef of rocks, where the iron sides of our wretched little steamer would be stove in by one blow, and we should then sink at once, for she had no compartments. The water was too deep to anchor in, and so we did for the best in making for more shallow water in shore.

The lady it was sad to see—poor thing, how she did cry! Only one other person besides the stoker behaved badly, a sailor passenger, who kept grumbling at the accident, and

croaking about his own personal inconveniences, when life was in danger, and a woman and children under our charge! He kept mumbling in this style as he walked from one end of the deck to the other—about three paces did it. On behalf of all of us I gave him such a hearty set-down in good sound English that he was ashamed of himself. Of course we scanned the horizon on all sides to see some friendly sail, and at length a steamer was seen, not that we could see her hull, but only a dense cloud of smoke, which also entirely obscured us from being noticed on board of her, as she was dead to windward. But when they observed our flag with the end knotted (the distress signal), we gladly saw them bearing down straight to our help. Now the lady began to cry for joy, and her two children, who had been very grave, but behaved well, cried in sympathy. There is nothing that either so unmans a man or so inspirits him to manly deeds as to see a woman crying. If he cannot possibly help her, then it is tenfold more agonizing to see her hopeless tears. But if he can by any daring pluck or muscle render any help, then, indeed, those very tears will nerve him to the utmost unless he be of soulless clay. We were at this time within 200 yards of the shoal, the warning buoy upon it being close under our lee; and the doubt was whether the steamer could reach us before we got on the rocks. The oldest sea captain and myself held one opinion as to how we should use our tarpaulin sail, and the two other captains held the reverse, but our plan was adopted.

I should mention that before we saw the steamer they wished me to launch the canoe, first to get ashore myself, and then to get help for the rest. But I said that would be useless, for the first danger was in the reef of rocks, and if we were to strike on them the canoe might be of use to us all, and especially to the lady and children; whereas if I now left the ship in her it would be some hours before I could get any help, and they agreed to this view. There was a further reason for my refusal to leave the steamer, for, suppose she had gone down while I was paddling away for assistance, it would have been quite impossible to convince the people on shore that I had not selfishly saved myself at the supreme moment of other people's death by sinking. The steamer Vidar seemed, however, to come to us with astonishing slowness, though she was under sail; and it turned out that she also was partially disabled. Our captain then took down our distress signal; but as this seemed to be a device for saving the paltry sum due to any other vessel that might put off to our relief, I ventured (after consulting the old "salt") to hoist it again. Stinginess is without excuse when applied to those who come to save life. Soon the Vidar was within hail, and her captain saw how near we were to the reef, and he, of course, did not wish to come nearer to it than he could help; but his friendly hand hove a rope on board, and in a few moments more we were bounding over the waves, towed back to Sönderburg on the 14th of September.

# CHAPTER XIX.

Old Rowlock — Foam — Isles of Denmark — Lollipops —
Back Doors.

THE shore was thronged again with gazers, many of
whom had seen us start in the morning; and the Prussian
soldiers laughed good-humouredly to find the Rob Roy
once more borne to land. As the weather now cleared up,
and the evening was before me, I determined not to lose it;
so, after a good dinner, the Rob Roy started off along the
channel which leads to Angustenburg, where we had some
hours of pleasant sailing, and landed in several places.

In a curious book lately published, 'Denmark in the Iron
Age,' it is mentioned that in a creek leading up from this
channel of Als Sund is the village of Nydam, where a very
curious relic was found embedded in the peat—a boat,
seventy-seven feet long and ten feet broad, with rowlocks
for twenty-eight oars. These rowlocks were of the shape
sketched at page 112, fig. 4; and it was very interesting to
observe, in the collection of modern boats at the Exhibition
in Stockholm, this form of rowlock precisely is still used in
some of the yawls on the Scandinavian coasts. The ancient
boat was very ancient, indeed, having been built, rowed,
stranded, and buried ages ago. The brave old planks seem
to have been sewn together with bark or ropes. Now it is set
up again, and preserved in the Museum at Flensborg; but

the feature that attracts me specially is the form of rowlock, for our canoe has no rowlocks at all.

At one of the quiet spots where we landed to look about, a sailor came who could speak English a little, and, looking at the boat's name on her bows, he said, "Ah, that Robe Roey, I had laese of him" (I have read of her). It was very strange to find the fame of the canoe extended to so obscure a harbour on a distant island in Denmark.

The time was one of great enjoyment. In the shallows, where the wind was most gusty, and an upset would be of no moment, I put on sail, and the sharp canoe skimmed along, or leaned over with the pressure of the breeze—ever fitful, and roaring through the forest on the bank—but the boat would not turn over. Such trials as these are of great service when they can be thoroughly and safely made, as they give you confidence in your boat, which, in time of sudden and unwished-for danger, is of principal importance, for it prevents you from being flurried. In one part of the channel very long weeds covered the surface, and gently resisting, smoothly yielded to my polished planks as the strong breeze urged the Rob Roy through them. But I confess to being rather suspicious of weeds, either to sail or to swim in. There is an uncertain and mysterious imagining as to what sort of unknown danger they contain or conceal; in fact, they are "uncanny," and it is very much the same with that white frothy foam which sometimes is six inches deep under a great waterfall. It hides the rocks, and you feel it is an unknown element, not watery enough to float on, but watery enough to drown.

In Sicily there is a vast plain of boiling mud, brown, hot, shining as it steams in the sun, and really this reeking, soft, uncomely slime looks far more terrible than Etna itself. The poet seized this idea well, who filled the infernal regions with waves of seething mud.

Let us paddle away from weeds and froth and mud, and go back to the pretty town again, with the setting sun glittering on its windows, and warming the red-tiled roofs of its neat little houses, each with a garden and summer-bower close to the edge of the sea.

Punctual and steady now comes a good strong English screw-steamer, the Vigilant, and by all means let us start again with confidence. She carried the canoe for nothing—thanks, good captain, may you soon be made an admiral!

For yachting the isles of Denmark are better than the Mediterranean. "Sailing among the Greek islands" is far nicer to read of than to do, as I know by experience—such bad anchorage, bad water, shifty winds, and long stupid calms, Greek pirates, quarantine, &c., &c. But up here in the fresh air of the north you are among free people and a sailor population, with good harbours and islands lively and lovely—up with the sail cheerily. Through mazes of them we come to Flensborg, which is high up a beautiful creek in the mainland—if, indeed, we can call any part of Denmark mainland—for the Eider cuts it right across.

Now, little Rob Roy, we have safely arrived, and you are to be mounted again on the top of a railway-carriage, which is the most secure of all modes of transit. A lady got into the same compartment with me, and four little boys, Germans, with blue caps and red bands, and chubby cheeks, all the caps and cheeks being of the same pattern, only of different sizes. They tugged away at lollipops for some miles, and generally imparted some to me—not all into my mouth—until friends at a station handed in four penny trumpets, and thenceforth the carriage was like a small slice of Greenwich Fair. The mamma soon saw that I liked children, and the other gentleman in the carriage (who turned out to be the President of Schleswig) was equally sensible, so she became very animated, being divided between motherly pride at the spirit and mischief of her small army and the desire to keep them within tolerable bounds. "Speak you English?" said their little sister, "and

French?" and when I said "Yes," she answered, "Speak moi." So we came to Altona, a suburb of Hamburg; and next day I launched on the great, dull, white-coloured Elbe, and paddled along the lines of tall ships, huge steamers, bright-coloured smacks, and boats of every rig and hue and nation in this fine, rich harbour.

But I had a mind to penetrate further and deeper; and unless you have gone up the narrow water-lanes of Hamburg, you have not well seen this strange old town. Lofty houses are on each side, built fantastically of rotten wood on rotten piles, resting in rotten mud, and without any approach along the edge of the water, and every probability of falling down. Thus for miles you penetrate into a third-rate Venice, with the crazy windows and dirty walls of the Jews' quarter marked by signs in Hebrew, and market-boats teeming with round cabbages blocking up the way. It would take many pages to describe the curious adventures of the Rob Roy in this *intramural* journey; but respect for the worthy Hamburgers requires me to suppress any account of how their dwellings looked from this novel point of view.

At every bridge there was a crowd to see the canoe, and then they ran round again to the next for another glimpse. Whenever I landed the people pressed so much that it was best at once to embark again. Yet this I will say, in all that long day's windings in the very worst parts of this great town, where to boyish minds it must have been tempting "to have a shie" at the canoe, not one missile was cast at the boat. Last year only once did the mischievous natives of a town cast stones, and that was at night, and in Holland. But after coming to England, I had not been a few hours upon the Thames before a lad in a barge threw a huge piece of coal at the Rob Roy. Truly Punch has depicted our manners, when he makes a lad tell his father—"There's a strange man a coming," and the father politely replies, "'Eave arf a brick at 'im."

# CHAPTER XX.

Hamburg Warriors — Mechanics' Institution — Popple on the Elbe — Trying a Tow — Dutchman, ahoy! — Too fast by far — Rude — "Mout" — Sleeping on Apples — Curious Voyage — Looking on — Lady Rowers — Grandmamma — Race with a Lady — Tongue-tied.

THE new part of Hamburg, rebuilt by the English after a great fire, has a handsome square round a central lake, on which are boats without number, and of every size, from a twelve-oar down to neat punts for teaching boys to row, and tiny steamers, and others with paddle-wheels turned by hand, for those special lunatics who attempt this thoroughly bad means of locomotion.[1]

A great crowd attracted my attention, and I found a street and bridges decorated, and staff-officers galloping about, until an infirm brass band *walked* forward at the head of the army of Hamburg, who are coming back to-day from the war; and see how the inhabitants are now welcoming them! Thousands line the streets, and throw garlands and roses to the trudging braves. Every man has a bouquet round his shako, a bunch of green in his gun-muzzle, a whole bush of it in his knapsack, and a girdle of all bright nosegays round his waist; and in the ranks, wildly mixed up with the soldiers, are their brothers and mothers, arm in arm. See that brown-faced young burgher, bronzed by the campaign, holding his needle-gun in one hand, while his other is round the neck of his fair—well, let us say cousin. Where has he come from, the honest-looking hero? What ensanguined plain are those laurels gathered in, and where are the one-armed or the limping wounded, and the dented shields of the dead? What, in fact, have these troops done to be feted and cheered and beflowered in this way? They had no fighting—but they were ready. Let us be glad they had not to fight; and I daresay not one of them is sorry.

The little canoe went up the creeks, and met boats full of mechanics going to dinner from their work. They sit in two rows on the sides of a great heavy barge, and each man has a short paddle, so that perhaps twenty are paddling, while another double row sits between them, inactive, the appearance of the whole being exactly like those great Indian canoes of the Pacific which are pictured in every book of missions or foreign travel. These men were immensely amused when the Rob Roy paddled up alongside, and claimed a sort of brotherhood closer than that of a boat with oars, in which you look one way and row the other.

I had intended to go to Berlin to see the entry—a really triumphant one—of the soldiers who won the brilliant victories of July and August; but, on thinking over the project, after all, it would only be a pageant, and we had come for a paddle, therefore I turned again to the Elbe, and started down this wide river for a three days' cruise. One bank is prettily wooded, and has a succession of neat houses, pleasure-boats, and gardens—the Richmond and Putney of the wealthy merchants here. After that both banks are more alike, though the north side is usually higher; and the islands of mud, rushes, and weeds, with winding, unctuous channels and high green embankments, spread out the river over miles of surface, while the south wind now raises a heavy sea on its grey-coloured surface. The canoe was soon careering on the powerful tide over the joyous waves, and carried by the stream with a whizzing noise through islets of stiff rushes,

or cutting across mud-banks, where no other boats could go. The wind was high, and waves toppled often over my sides—not at all dangerous, but still somewhat troublesome, because each separate wave has to be dealt with, and though, after months of experience there is an instinct created in the body which enables you to paddle on without looking at the water; yet in broken water there is a disadvantage when a long distance has to be accomplished, for it is evident that your boat travels further in going from one point to another, up and down and round so many little liquid hills, than on a smooth, level lake.

It was charming to toss about while the great ships passed, and the fleet of fisher-boats bowing to the breeze. Each of them had a look at me coming closer, and a nod and a smile and a cheer came from many. My dinner (providently brought from the hotel) was taken under an island, where I found a poor woman gathering mussels; and when I gave the empty wine-bottle into her withered hand she blessed me ever so long. Soon the wind freshened, and I laid hold of a boat towing after a brig, but my rope slipped, and the brig was going too fast to be caught again. Resolved, however, to have a "tow" (just because I had missed getting it—so perverse is free nature), we signalled to a Dutch cutter to luff up, and the Rob Roy was speedily made fast to the square stern of the "Neptun." The worthy skipper had his two sons on board, and was carefully teaching the boys how to sail the tub they were to inherit; and he pointed out all the beacons and currents as we scurried along. It was a very strange mode of travelling this, surely, to sit steering a canoe on the wide, grey, cold river, while it was pulled at a rapid pace in the two wake waves astern of this great smack, with the windows of its stern staring at me, and the captain's wife sitting aloft, her profile very Dutch from my point of view.

The wind freshened rapidly, and it was no easy matter to keep the Rob Roy straight when the sea got high. The Dutch boys grinned at me through the little ports; and other vessels as they passed were all duly informed by my good skipper of the odd fish he had caught.

Excellent man, he was truly proud of his post, and his whole soul wrapt in one desire, that his clumsy barge might beat one still more clumsy, now sailing neck and neck with him, about a mile to the north. I quite entered into his feeling about this race, and admired his courtesy in stopping at my request, when so much glory might be hazarded by the time lost in the act, and he had the additional labour of towing me along when attached.

But when he had fairly beaten the other Mynheer von Dunck, and when he had received an approving smile from me, with a nod over my shoulder at the beaten rival, the wind had really become so fresh that my being dragged along was far more dangerous than dignified; in fact the whole arrangement gave incessant work in steering, for one yard of a swerve would have instantly engulfed me; and it would be a wretched end for the Rob Roy to founder behind a Dutchman, while the dripping captain would wail on the waves. So we determined at the next lull between the squalls to cast off and be free; and I sung out to the skipper to receive a bottle I pitched to him of the finest essence of coffee from Fortnum and Mason's, which would make him at least twenty cups.

My directions about the proper use of this being given out in very bad Dutch, and in a roaring breeze, were, no doubt, so intelligible that the man probably drank off the whole bottle at a draught—and who can tell with what result?

At all events, now we are free. In a waste of waves, the river as broad as the Thames at Sheerness, and evening coming on, and thirty miles accomplished, and low, flat banks far off, almost unseen—what grand and wild and unshackled feelings came into Rob Roy's mind. But after an hour or two there arose the unmistakable and indescribable sensation that the tide was changing, and the low mud banks might soon prevent me from getting in anywhere; so we determined to run for the nearest estuary, and chance it, as so many times we had done before.

At the head of the inlet we saw a few housetops over the lofty embankment, and masts of some sloops; and on landing there was a coast-guardsman, who insisted on. knowing what we had on board.

The fellow was gruff, and actually unbuttoned my bag of clothes; and I told him indignantly that this mode of examination was illegal (they are bound to let the owner open the luggage), and then he wished to peer into my sponge-bag, containing my meagre toilette, one small brush, two inches broken off a comb, a tooth-brush, and a Testament. He was determined, and so was I; and I resisted forcibly, and told him I would shove off and go adrift into the night, if he insisted on making a fool of himself. Poor wretch! He probably had caught a stranger for the first time in his long and dull service, so his eagerness was excusable; and next day we made it up, and were good friends when I had sketched his portrait, so as to be highly complimentary, and, therefore, only rather ugly. So I mounted the bank, and the bystanders seemed awed by the traveller's air—partly of cool dignity—partly of general madness; so they made no resistance, but carried the boat into a room full of apples, then fetched twelve chairs in, and a bed was made on them—the only one for some weeks that was really long enough to stretch in, and where there was no fear of narrow sheets, for, of course, I slept in my clothes. People soon came in from the houses, far and near, and the room was full of the population of Billenberg; and my traveller's tale was told, and the pictures shown, and the magnesium light—all the old, old scene, so very interesting to see, though dull, perhaps, to read of; for there were new features in it every time. Here, for instance, came a fine boy of twelve, back from school. His delight at being shown the canoe was truly amusing. He had a "boating mind," and revelled in the new sight. His proud mother produced an English reading-book from his knapsack (even the girls wear knapsacks for their school-books), and I gave him an hour's lesson in English gratis, amid profound silence from the group of sailors, farmers' servants, and hinds. When he read the word "mouth" as "mout," and I had fairly hammered the difficult "th" into his quick young brain, he jumped up and cried to his mother, "I knew it was so; I was sure my teacher of English at school doesn't know how to speak it right. Here this Herr says ' mouth,' and my teacher tells me to say 'mout.'"

The whole affair reminded me of a time when I was sailing by myself, years ago, on the embouchure of the Thames, and my little boat was caught on a sandbank, where I had to pass six hours alone in my ship—not eleven feet long—on a hot day, waiting for the tide, and with only a book of logarithms to amuse myself with (it was for carrying my chart in); and thus being delayed had to put in for the night at a solitary house, where there was no one but the captain of a coal-brig. Still, by keeping him upon the subject of coal and colliers, we had a very interesting chat—a tune on one string, indeed, but perfectly played.

Off to my chair-bed, and now the apples had been decently collected into one corner, so I was able to pick out the most juicy ones; and, as no pretence of water-basin or such luxuries had been placed in the room, and I was thirsty, it would not be fair to inquire how many, or how many dozen, apples I munched while my log was noted up, and a few sketches added to a very curious collection, filling two volumes already in this tour.

Good health and hard exercise make days and nights like this quite enjoyable. To me they are infinitely more so than the tedious round of Swiss hotels, with only the place changed, but not the people.

Next morning I launched again, and with vigour and a good cup of coffee on board, we paddled on to Glückstadt, a large village in Holstein, one of the quaintest and most old-fashioned you can see. Royal progress to the hotel—we need not tell this again. Then for a long walk on the great sea-wall, to gaze on this splendidly rich country, full of good comfortable houses, teeming gardens, sleek oxen, winding canals, and fine old trees. Little wonder that such a prize has been fought for with sword and pen for now four hundred years. Five hundred Prussians were coming here next day.

At the end of our walk we came to the mouth of the River Stoer, which (according to Chauchard's map) rises within a mile or two of the east side of Holstein, quite close to Kiel, and curiously enough runs the whole whole way across the country, some sixty miles, before it can satisfy its whim as to finding a proper exit.[2]

The people and the place seemed to be so interesting

that I resolved to make a canoe voyage into this strange country; but this was by no means so easy a matter as might be supposed, for the navigation is intricate, and the language unutterable; but then the Rob Roy is not to be stopped by difficulties; and when it was given out in the town that "the Englishman" was to sail up the Rhyn river, and get on the net of canals which go forty miles into this flat land, every one was astir; and, moreover, the Hamburg papers had told them what the canoe was, and where she had been to.

The crowd to see the start was exceedingly strange to behold, for now-a-days I have such *sang froid* on these occasions that all my attention can be given to looking and listening—the perfection of mind for really enjoying a tour.

We still had some illustrated periodicals left in the sea-chest of our purser. These were given carefully to such of our visitors as could read German or Danish; and in all cases they were received with much gratitude. A gentleman at the hotel said the host had gone to Hamburg to attend a Freemasons' meeting; and he asserted that Freemasons did not believe in the Ascension of our Lord. This led to a very useful conversation about the central fact of the world's history—the cardinal point of revelation, which is, of course, the Resurrection of Jesus Christ. I had read with deep interest Mr. Westcott's book—"The Gospel of the Resurrection;" and here in this far-off village was an excellent opportunity for using some of the deep and truthful thoughts in that, book, which were received and discussed with much mind and heart by my friend, a clever Dane.

The river led through a perfect series of market-gardens, full of the most magnificent fruits and vegetables, and with every foot of ground tilled to the water's edge, and pear-trees drooping over the canoe; capital sweet pears they were. Then we came, after some miles, to a village, where the school-children rushed out en masse upon the rustic bridge, screaming joyously, and every house was emptied. Next came the fishers' boats, and then the vegetable-boats, with women rowing them, and then the Rob Roy emerged from trees and gardens among the verdant pastures, with tall reeds and pink clover brushing my blue paddle-blades, and wondering cows staring, but not convinced. The evening sun reddened this glorious landscape, and the ripple of the long deep pools flapped against the oaken sides of my little boat, which seemed to smile at small waves like these, after the rough tossing of yesterday. You see what endless and pleasant variety there is in a tour of this sort.

In a lonely place we came to an enclosure with seven great bulls in it. On seeing the boat they ran to me, snorted, bellowed, danced about. I splashed their faces, and rushed at them through the reeds, till the beasts were furious, and charged into the water; but I could always keep my boat a foot or so from their horns, and splash their great broad brows. Then they retreated and ran over the field, with tails in the air, and ploughing up the soft ground with their horns; and at last they fell to boxing each other with their heads.

In one village I noticed a man among the crowd who at once ran away, evidently to bring some one to see; and he presently returned, carrying upon his back no less a person than his grand-mother. Her position was by no means a comfortable one, for he held her by her two wrists over his shoulders; and his fine young face was ruddy with delight that he had brought her in time to see. With due respect to hoary heads, I approached the lady and made a deep salaam; and she stared at me over her grandson's shoulder, evidently not at all satisfied about the arrangement of things in general.

The country has several great dikes, with roads on their tops, just as in Holland; and the size, neatness, and solidity of the houses very much astonished and pleased me. The

Rob Roy meandered for hours up one canal after another into the most out-of-the-way places, where never foreigner was seen. Sometimes I went into tunnels—but of course without any notion of where they might lead to; and so there suddenly appeared in some lonely but busy farmyard an Englishman in a canoe, grey as to his dress, and beaming with smiles.

In another part of the river we overtook a great fat market-woman rowing a heavy boat up a very narrow channel, and with a heap of empty baskets on it, which served the good dame well for a sail. Instantly I made chase; but the lady did not yield to let the canoe pass, so we had a chat, rowing alongside, until we became capital friends, though not one word that was said had the very least meaning to the person addressed. I was reminded on this occasion of the strictures in a review of my book of last year's voyage. All the notices of the press were kind to the book as a new tale of new journeying; but one paper gave a sharp rebuke to the man who dared to travel where the language was one he did not know. Only think what a linguist this critic must become before he attempts a voyage such as we have described! First he must learn Norwegian, then Swedish, then back to Danish, then Slesvig *patois*, next German, then Platt (on the Elbe), and then at least four dialects of Holstein. While he tarries at home ten years, till he can talk all these like a dragoman, the Rob Roy will have merrily paddled over the rest of Europe.

## END NOTES

1—For many years Spain has claimed the merit of having made the first steamboat; and it was said to be described in 1543 in a letter written by the inventor, Blasco de Garay. Having had occasion to inspect this letter officially, in the archives at Simancas, I can state that it does not mention steam at all, but describes a boat with paddle-wheels turned by two hundred men.

2—A lake marked near this in old maps seems to be no longer existing.

# CHAPTER XXI.

The Wizard — Hard Times — Buffeting — Son of a Sponge
— Attack by Natives — White Lies — Pyramid Wave —
Dry — His Mother.

SKETCHES are a language universal; so these, at least,
were always available for my evening's entertainment of the
wondering people I had, to sit with sometimes, and yet
could not speak to. The gravest seniors relaxed into smiles
at a lively picture, and, as for the boys and girls, their
delight was boundless. Oh, the fresh, merry ring of a young
throat laughing. Heavily-afflicted adult he is, and tame and
dry and withered his heart's sympathy, who does not enjoy
it.

On several occasions much additional amusement was
given to the natives by a man on board the Rob Roy, who
showed some conjuring tricks—all of a simple kind as
regards apparatus, but difficult to perform, until you know
how. Lifting a man seated on a chair with one hand; passing
a loaf through a straw hat without touching it; raising a
stick with the open palm of the hand flat above it; creeping
into a wine bottle, or threading a string through a pair of
scissors; all these were novelties, and were fully appreciated
by the gaping spectators.

Another favourite puzzle was sometimes left to a whole
community to solve; or the passengers on a steamer's deck
were set to unravel it; and perhaps the problem may here be
proposed also, with the assistance of the sketch on page 67,

figure 2. There is no "catch" or deception in it, but all is fair and honour bright; and when you have found it out you can do it at once, and will never forget the way, and always be proud of this discovery.

Take a strong needle, and place it in a pocket-handkerchief, so that P is the point, E the eye, and the parts P A and B E are on one side of the handkerchief, while the part A B (the dotted line) is on the other side. Then put a thread through the eye E, and under A P, and knot it at K, so forming a loop, which must not, however, be long enough to be slipped over the point P, even when drawn tightly.

You are now required to extricate the needle and thread from the handkerchief without breaking the needle or the thread or the knot, or pricking your fingers or losing your temper.

All these jokes and riddles are well enough on shore or in fair weather, but now we have a practical puzzle of a far different kind. A thick drizzling rain, wind whistling, and muddy waves tossing on the Elbe were before me; and we must paddle through them from Glückstadt, or we could not catch the steamer to Heligoland, and save our plans from being quite disjointed.

Two or three times I was inclined to give up the project. The steamer would come, they said, along the other side of the river some time between ten and eleven o'clock; and I must start from this side, some miles distant, before nine o'clock, so as to pull over the bank in the middle, where an angry sea was rolling, with the tide one way, and the wind opposing it. But once having resolved to go, we called for the last time at the telegraph-office, to see if any answer had come to the telegram of the preceding day, which had asked the captain if he would stop his steamer in the sea for the canoe—for unless he would stop, all the labour and the two hours' wetting would be in vain. No answer had come (though prepaid); and the boatmen all said this steamer would not stop for passengers in such weather. I then engaged a pilot-boat, which would sail further up the river, and hail the steamer some way above me, to point out the Rob Roy in the waves; and while the crowd wondered at it all, I pushed out from the little harbour into the great, white, rolling Elbe.

Buffeting and boxing the waves, the Rob Roy behaved nobly; and the pilots scudding alongside with two reefs in their sail, could not cease their wonder at the little thing's steadiness. "Didn't I take that big breaker well?" "First-rate," they shouted; and then came the rollers on the bank, the white-crested hillocks that puzzle one so much, because, when rain is driving into your face, and a great splash of foam comes slap in your eyes, just at that very instant you ought to be most distinct in your policy, and keenly alive to every wave. An hour of hard work, in which my right arm had to bear the brunt of it, and slightly "gave," or felt strained, and then we glided into quiet water, where we could wait until the smoke of the approaching steamer might appear on the leaden-coloured horizon; but then I must prepare for another dash into the broken waves.

So we ran the canoe into a mass of tall reeds, to see if she had got any water. There were only three "spongefuls." Then the sponge became a subject of interest; it was my fourth sponge, and the smallest, for three had been stolen. Ostlers at inns cannot resist a sponge, just as men at a club are lax in their morality about umbrellas. And while we pondered on the metaphysics of kleptomania and sponges, and the pleasant theory that a sponge, instead of an oyster, might have been my great-great-great-grandfather, by the Darwin line, twenty-four times removed, the swell rose and fell sleepily among the tall reeds, which only rustled; else there was blank silence. Very soon I heard a sharp conversation between the pilots and a number of men on the bank, who could not now see me among the reeds, but who had crowded down to the spot. Suddenly the pilot called out, "Come away, sir! Come away, sir, instantly! The

men are going to catch you!" These natives had watched us riding over the waves, and could not make out what all this meant; but the pilots had told them I was a wild Chinaman escaped from a ship, and that they were in chase of me. Away went the duped natives, and presently brought clubs, sticks, and a great hatchet. They were a clumsy and ignorant set; but I thought it was all meant for fun, so up rose the captain of the Rob Roy, his head only over the reed tops, and his face grimacing, and paddle whirled aloft, just as an escaped Chinaman would doubtless do, with wild shrieks as an accompaniment. The natives became frantic; but there was only mud there—no stones to be had. Then the pilots, to humour the joke, sailed after me, and splashed with their oars and lowered their sail and shouted aloud; while the canoe darted here and there on the water, wildly, but always eluded their grasp, and sought refuge again in the reeds.

How different must have been the two stories of the same facts related that night on one side and the other of the Elbe, by the pilots and the armed natives of the reedy island—like the chat at a Cabinet council after a debate on the estimates, compared with the talk of the deluded minority discussing their defeat. Say, clever casuist, when may we deceive our neighbour? In jest, perhaps—but then these natives, at least, were in solid earnest; for they vigorously persevered for half-an-hour, even in the rain. "We must not deceive when it is for our own interest?" but the exercise was of great benefit to me, for I might else have been chilled.

As the smoke of the steamer gradually neared us, I found it was a fine, large, three-masted vessel, once the Britannia, which used to sail to America, but now called the Heligoland; and when it was seen that she had her sails set, I felt sure she would not stop to take up a passenger, and spend time and trouble about his boat. But the pilots hailed, and the captain had read of the canoe, and the Rob Roy I placed right before his nose, and so all the passengers ran forward to see the little skiff, as it rose now and then from the trough of a wave.

It was a time of suspense, when the great black hull came looming on, and the foam at its bows and paddles showed its speed. All at once, the paddles, so white with foam, became red; they had stopped. How I did shout "Hurrah!" "Thanks, captain, thanks."

Then before me, in this hotch-potch jumble of waves and mist and rain, there rose up two great pointed crests, where the steamer's swell crossed the waves of the Elbe, and these must both be passed.

A long wave you can calculate upon, and you soon come to know how to lean over in passing it, however obliquely. But when a wave is of the pyramid shape, and you must cross its very point, with a current bearing you sideways, it is utterly impossible to predict whether you will be on the steep slope of the right or left, and whether you will not be on the one side going up, and the other in the descent. The difficulty of dealing instantaneously with such a doubtful matter must be obvious.

Mrs. or Miss Header, were you ever poised on the cold shining edge-point of a three- sided wave? If so, you need no more explanation.

As the little canoe came rapidly to the first of these waves, it was so much higher and sharper than usual that I felt—"Here is the Rob Roy's grave. If in the upset now certain I let go my boat and hold by my paddle (the proper course in other cases) the steamer people will save only me and let the canoe drift away, for why should they stop for her ? Therefore I must loosen my hold on the paddle and cling to the boat, however difficult, for then they will rescue us both. But how?"—and, looking up (this the last thought vivid on my brain), "by that boat hanging on the davits, I see it is ready." All this was as a flash of instant thought, and then a thud of angry muddy water struck my cheek and knocked off my straw hat (luckily secured by a cord), and then down, down, down we swooped, and again a blow, a twist, and a squeeze, and both waves were past, and I could hear the end of the word "bravo-o-o!" as the mate shouted loud from the steamer above.

Right swiftly leaped I by the side of the vessel, and a last spiteful wave followed me running up the steps, and embraced me with one cold grasp about the loins—a drench to say "good-bye." The Rob Roy is safe aboard, and I dive into the steamer's cabin, still trembling with a certain thrill of excitement, of hard work done—a feat accomplished—three days saved—dry clothes putting on, and all the time repeating over and over, "I never will again board a steamer in a gale."

Presently my cabin-door opened, and a raw, vulgar lad looked in, holding his hand to shake mine, and claiming acquaintance as a Scotchman, though his dialect was so excessively broad that we took him for a German. This boy of nineteen has come straight from the island of Lewis, in the Hebrides, to Heligoland, to take charge of the fishery. "Where do you come from?" said I. "I'm frae Logiemurchie." "And what places have you ever seen?" "Weel, I hae been at Stornoway, an' Aberdeen, an' Dundee, and—and Aberdeen." "And for whom are you going to work?" "For Mr. Bell. D'ye ken Mr. Bell?— No ken Mister Bell of London? Hoot, I thought ye'd ken him. He's a maun wi' white hair."

There was an opportunity of having a very useful and uncommonly plain-said conversation with this young fellow, sent so far and so soon as a green Caledonian among the rough and dissipated people of the North Sea harbours. He took it well what was spoken. If a man has a mother, and he is away from her, and a stranger speaks of her, it must be a right down hard heart that does not take it well and softly.

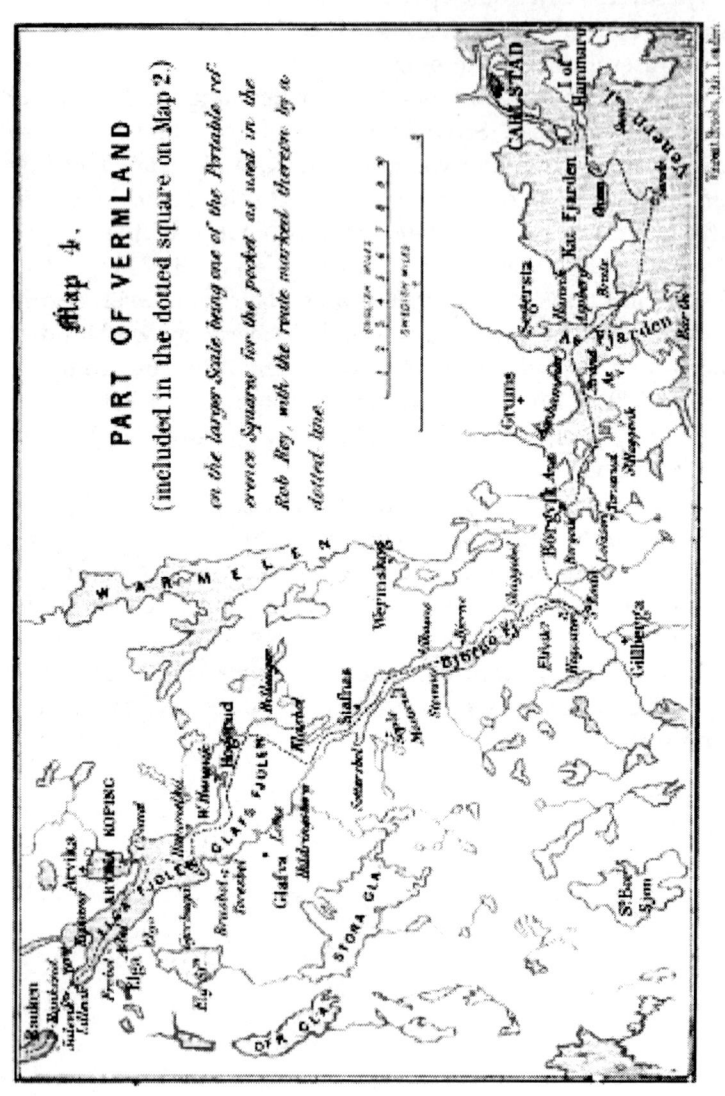

Map 4.

PART OF VERMLAND

(included in the dotted square on Map 2.)

on the larger Scale being one of the Portable reference Squares for the pocket as used in the Rob Roy, with the route marked thereon by a dotted line.

194

# CHAPTER XXII.

HERE before us is the little ruddy island of Heligoland, with just enough soil to plant the brave old English flag upon, a miniature colony of the all-wide British Empire; and a very curious, interesting place, by no means easy to describe; but we may try. Take one of those flat richly-red tiles, which has bright green moss on its level surface, and chop off an odd three-cornered piece an inch broad and two inches long, and put it on a blue slate, which will be the sea; the bit of tile itself answers to the grassy level top and sharp vertical sides of red rock, and along the shorter side and at its foot you have a cluster of houses, white, blue, grey, of every colour and shape, huddled picturesquely close together.

We land from, huge boats, being carried on men's backs through the last rolling wave; and suddenly we are on English soil, but with scarce one English sight or sound beside us. The swarthy sailors are gabbling a perfectly new language without a grammar, not written, but still their own. Their fathers had the same when they victualled fleets in the days of Van Tromp, and harried many a hapless crew in wintry nights lost in the wide, wide sea. All these people together are but 2,300 souls; then other thousands, nearly all Germans, come here to bathe, crowding every morning to cross to Dune Island, with its pearly strand and emerald waves. Then they will take a puff and a cafe in the pavilion, and a walk on the plank promenade, and a climb up the one stair that leads with two hundred steps to the Upper Town, where, from the neat, clean balcony of a logis perched on the rock, you can look over far-off water, and see the broad golden band unrolled upon it from the full moon as it rises slowly. British soil; but where is the Briton? Why, there is scarcely one Englishman in the place except the Governor; and His Excellency is a right good one to make up for this scarcity. He was very kind to me, being at once a canoe man and a Guardsman; and as the Rob Roy voyage of last year was on his table, he needed no introduction from the paddling visitor.

During the three days we spent here the sensation of "incongruity" was most powerful. A charming island quite neglected. An English land full only of foreigners. A rock with wooden houses. A poor town with rich visitors. A splendid beach without a pier. The airiest of nests with drains so foul. Crowds of thinking Germans, but only one book-shop. Planks for pavement where no tree grows. One church, one school, a good brass band, and a beautiful glee chorus. What a neat, little, pretty, open, confined, old-fashioned, interesting, neglected place to be sure! A huge fortune might readily be made by investing capital here. This little ruby in the green sea could be set off with gold as a gem.

Heligoland, not so large as Hyde Park, is about fifty miles from the mouth of the Elbe, and sixty from Bremerhaven on the Weser.

Some assert, others deny, that the rocks are rapidly corroding, or, at any rate, disappearing.

Certainly the slips or falls of rocks in many places seem very recent; and the water is coloured ruddy for a long distance round the island. Also, on a map of Chauchard's, published in 1800, we may observe that the contour of the island "called Heylegeland" is given. Moreover, this map of seventy years ago does not indicate the sandy island of Dyne, or Dune (pronounced nearly Deeny), which is due east of the other.

The water in Heligoland is derived from large tanks, which collect the rain from the roofs of the houses.

The name, signifying Holy Island, is said to be derived from the fact that the Saxon goddess Phoseta was worshipped here.

The inhabitants seem very fond of the little place; but I confess that there were two feelings always present in my mind during my brief visit—the sensation of "Falling over the edge," and of "Can't get out,"—both of which one recognises as the well-known staples of nightmare horrors.

Should you mean to stop here for the winter, make up your mind to get letters by a sailing-boat a few times in the month, and salt meat and salt fish—that which is dried before your eyes, flapping about on strings in the rope-walk Regent Street, and in all the other streets; or you may rise early in the morning, and put up your net to catch one of the woodcocks that fly over the town. Many curious birds, not seen anywhere else so easily, stop to rest at Heligoland, which is thus an excellent station for the ornithologist.

The new Constitution, dating from 1864, has some features worth noticing, as the form of Colonial government most lately sanctioned by Britain, and for a possession so compact and so minute. These may be gathered from the ordinances enacted in the island, and approved by Parliament at home. The Government is conducted by a Governor, who is also Commander-in-Chief (of any future army and navy), and by a "Legislative Council" of twelve appointed by the Crown, and of twelve elected by the colonists (with a small property-qualification for franchise), who together form the "Combined Court," and from whom the Governor selects five as an "Executive Council." The Crown may disallow laws enacted by the Combined Court, and enact others, which, if involving taxation, must be ratified by the Court. The Governor appoints judges, officers, and ministers, and may remit fines and extend pardons. He may also suspend any member of the Legislative Council. There are three stipendiary magistrates and a Court of Session appointed by the Governor as an Appeal Court and to try civil cases (with a jury if it is demanded). Three-fourths of the jury in civil cases, and all of them in criminal cases, must agree to a verdict.

The proceedings at elections are conducted by four "Quartermasters" for the "two grand districts" of the island. These are pilot officers, and form "an amicable Court as regards wrecking and pilot cases." Strict rules provide for the duties and rewards of boats saving vessels in distress, and prohibit the bargaining for salvage in such cases on the hard terms often exacted in old times. The clergyman appoints a churchwarden, and another is chosen from the Legislative Council. These two manage "the poor house" and send round "the monthly voluntary poor book," and inspect the repairs of the church and the school buildings. Every child between the age of six and fourteen must go to school, being compelled by the police, and may be fined 7s. 6d. for a day's absence. The school is managed by a "Directing Committee," including the clergyman and members of the Combined Court. Parents who are impudent to teachers may be fined 15s. "For the purpose of heating the school-rooms, each child, according to the old-established custom, shall bring daily one piece of turf, not cut in halves or quarters, but according as it is sold on the island." "Should the cold become so excessive that more firing is required, or that coals become necessary, application shall be made by the teacher, through the superintending clergyman, to the Directing Committee, who will act according to their judgment, and report in their accounts to the Finance Committee of the Combined Court." The routine for fetching a scuttle of coals being thus particular, it may well be supposed that the regulations for each hour of instruction of the four classes in the school are very distinct. For the older children five hours a week are devoted to religious teaching, and two to English; while the other classes have also their time apportioned. Taxation "shall be arranged according to the personal means of each inhabitant of the colony," by the Combined Court.

There are few duties on imports—about twopence a bottle for spirits, and three-halfpence for wine. The oyster fishery is conducted by the Government, as the inhabitants neglected this profitable work; and the regulations for this enterprise occupy the paragraphs of the last Ordinance we need allude to, and so ends our legal study tonight.

In the cool grey morn we float off early to the sandy isle of Dune, with its swelling waves of purest green and beach of sparkling white. Whole families go in great boats for a long day's stay, the mothers and nurses to knit and gossip, while the children bathe and dig, or sail their toy boats, catch crabs, roll in the soft sand, squall, fight, or dine under the verandah of the cafe, as children ought to do. Heligoland lives by Dune. If the sand were to be washed away the houses on the red rock opposite would be all " to let."

A great hubbub was raised about this patch of sand last year, by some one asserting that rabbits had been imported here, and that these would burrow the heart out of poor Dune, and the waves would then sweep away its mangled remains. I started in search of these rabbits, being determined to eye out at least one of the rapacious creatures; but not one was to be found anywhere.

In one of the boats full of children I observed a toy rocking-horse; and it seems that no horse or beast of burden has ever been on the island; where, also, the milk for your breakfast is that of the little steep tethered on the cliffs, and fed by old women in red gowns and huge bonnets.

To move at all in Heligoland you must either walk up and down stairs—*the* stairs by which alone the upper surface of the rock can be reached—or you must go in a boat, This supposes, of course, that you have already promenaded along the main street, which is a "rope-walk," with a man engagingly spinning a yarn beside you, and moving backwards with a great bunch of tow round his waist. But let us, therefore, embark.

The boatmen regarded me with jealousy and a tinge of contempt. At first they felt sure this Rob Roy cockle-shell was a mere English toy, and that it might float in the sun, but would be swamped at once by a wavelet in the breeze. Very soon they found she was faster than their big, clumsy boats; and when we got out in the full-drawn swell, and the canoe bounded over the water, and round and round their labouring boats joyously, their notions were changed, and wonder filled them, instead of ridicule. This bathing-place of Dune is one of the prettiest little *bijoux* ever was seen, and we enjoyed a half-hour there very much.

Next day we determined to paddle round the main island; and the Governor and his wife, "Excellenza," as I heard her called, came in their boat, manned by a fine crew, rigged out in true British-sailor uniform, and so we set off in a lovely calm. The cliffs were studded with visitors perched aloft to see; and they slowly followed us high up while we skimmed over the long and gentle swells below. The canoe could, of course, run about here as it pleased her, and she dipped into little bays, or shot through arches in the rock, or peeped into darksome caves where the water gurgled far in, and then rushed out, afraid of the blackness.

This was indeed a holiday trip for the Rob Roy; moving with a quiet and almost processional pace, and new things every moment to be seen. How about the fell principle of "nationalities," and the Pole-Magyar-Czech-Celt doctrine, that "the peoples" ought to govern themselves? In plainer words—is it right for England to rule Heligoland? Is it

better, juster, and more humane for us to keep as Governor there an Englishman, thoroughly anxious to maintain rights, liberty, and order, or to cast the little isle adrift, like an open boat at sea, without a week's provisions, and where sharks and Bismarcks do abound? The islanders here are not at all Germans; yet they must know that if they were cast off by England, they would be snapped up in a month by Prussia, and their green grass would be soon cut into glacis, and forts would replace the hotels. Let them beware of the fate of the Ionian Islands, who exchanged happy freedom under the broad aegis of Britannia for a dull servitude under the brigand rule of Greece.

Gambling is allowed in this island, and to hear this startled me; but it was explained that there is an "enormous national debt" of £7000, and as England, which receives nothing from the island, objected to pay this, and so to stop the *rouge et noir* (a main source of revenue), there was nothing for it but to allow the people to gamble on for eight weeks every year until 1871, when it is believed that the debt will be liquidated.

Steaming off into the green sea in a steamer with "twin-screws," the red cliffs of the island became blue in the distance, and then other isles appeared. They are part of the chain of banks that girds the coast all round the north of Holland and the Zuider Zee. One of these is Norderney—a name to be inflected with a sturdy drop on the last syllable; and this is another bathing-place, quite a fashionable resort, if one may judge from the frequent advertisements about it. A new submarine telegraph-cable has just been laid from this island to Lowestoft; and a good deal is to be seen and learned at this part of the world from these out-of-the-way places one has not even heard the names of yet in England. [Mental resolve on board the Rob Roy—"A run about this part of the world would be an excellent trip for another year."][1]

My fellow-passengers were a judge from Lübeck, with his two daughters, all speaking English well, and an Austrian nobleman, who had a long talk with me in French about education and lodging-houses and priests and timber and religion; and now we are arrived at Bremerhaven, where the Rob Roy enters a third-rate inn, with a courteous host who would place the canoe in the bowling-green; but as we found the tide was still running up the river, my boat was launched, and her well-washed sails unfurled on the broad, sedate Weser, and hie away! we are off again for one more cruise as of yore. This was a long and delightful trip, but with little to see that can be put on paper. Indeed, a very great deal of the enjoyment of this voyage is of that peculiar kind which though felt very strongly sounds weak to tell.

How seldom it is that in ordinary travelling we can say with truth, "I wish this hour to be many hours just so—this day to be a week as it is now." The test of satisfaction is that you are not sated when it is done; and certainly in this most interesting cruise I have over and over again wished the present "now" to be much prolonged.

The hotel was called the "Hanover," for the dot of land it is built on was part of that kingdom; but now, of course, it is "Bismarcked" into the Fatherland. It was curious to visit these little bits of various territories in one afternoon's paddle, especially as in a very short time they were all incorporated in Prussia.

What will be the effect of all these changes on the religious state and education of Germany? Perhaps while things are thus in transition it may be interesting to consider some particulars, which 1 obtain from a pamphlet just published anonymously, but understood to be written by a well-known traveller. It is called "The Church of Rome under Protestant Governments;" and some of the most important conclusions arrived at by the writer, after a personal investigation last year in Prussia, we have given in the Appendix.

A mere traveller's views about the deeper politics, civil and ecclesiastical, of a foreign people, are very likely to be erroneous. Even in our own land, the great questions of Reform, of Free-Church, and of Popery, require the study for years of a resident in England, Scotland, and Ireland, while India cannot be comprehended without the loss of your liver.

But one thing does strongly arrest us in looking at Prussia—how quiet are the religious sections.

It is, however, the calm of stagnation. There is little ferment, for the yeast is dead. The believers do not believe even enough to tremble. Is anybody in downright earnest about religion, or is the Apostle's injunction turned upside down, as if it were "First peaceable, then pure?"

This may be a pleasant, but certainly it is a dangerous state. Christ did not come to settle us in this way. Better far, with all its turmoil and discord, is the restlessness of England awake, and the ship of truth tossing in the waves and storms from all sides—Irish Papists and rebels, Oxford Apists and rituals, the priests and the ribbonmen of the church and the chapel.

The wind is high, but the ship will not sink, for there is One who is Highest walking on the waves.

END NOTES
1—Fulfilled in the summer of 1871 with great satisfaction.

# CHAPTER XXIII.

River Geste— Roast Beef— Horrid!— Salt Beef.

BUT the log of the Rob Roy must float along the water, and not become fixed on the platform either of politics or religion; so we are embarked again in the canoe for a trip up the River Geste, where the usual reception awaited her; and the pleasure of the Hanoverians was all the same as if their kingdom had not just been swallowed alive. Nine-tenths of the common people, indeed, seem to care very little as to who rules them. But we may well pity the poor blind King of Hanover, who has built the splendid docks at Bremerhaven, and now sees them quietly annexed by Prussia, and six men-of-war lying there, all with the Berlin flag. "Sees" them, I say, for he says he "sees" always; and, with the smallest-minded vanity, he insists upon being treated in private as if he were not stone-blind.

At length, as we loll on the waves where the Geste falls into the Weser, there sails down towards us the Falke steamer, in. which we are going to England.

All the passengers seem to know the Rob Roy well. It has filled paragraphs in their papers until they have been pestered by it, and they (and perhaps you) have voted it to be a bore. Still, the ladies on board the steamer, and the ladies on shore who come to see them off, are charmed with the canoe, and they cluster around it and pat its travelled sides. "How interesting! To see, indeed, the real Rob Roy canoe! Who would have thought it?" Ay, who indeed!

Hoist her up, good Captain, and you, Mr. Mate, give a tender, helping hand. Now she is carefully stowed aboard, keel uppermost, and the lowing of 290 great fat bullocks soon announces what sort of fellow-passengers we have to carry. Poor things, they are packed together in three tiers, one over the other.

Oh, the roast beef of old England! The sad twinges borne by that "undercut" before we eat the sirloin in London—the Slesvig thumps to drive it to a pen on the

Weser, the German whacks to force it up a gangway on board, the haulings and shoves, the wrenchings of horns and screwing of tails to pack it in the hold of the steamer, the hot thirsty days and cold hungry nights of the passage, the filth, the odour, the feverish bellowing, and the low dying moan at each lurch of the sea—who can sum up these for one bullock's miseries? and there are thousands every day. Who dare tell them, or ought to tell them, unless these cruelties can be stopped and these sufferings put an end to? But they can and they will be relieved, for good and wise men have taken this subject in hand.[1]

Our captain, and indeed the crew and the drovers, did not appear to be heartless in the matter. It is the system and plan of shipping cattle at all which must be amended. To put suffering, dying bullocks in the same steamer with passengers is utterly a mistake. The vessel cannot be used for both purposes without being unfit for either, since the two are quite incompatible.

If a wretched bullock becomes at all sea-sick, he speedily dies. If he is even weaker than his unhappy companions, and lies down after two days and nights of balancing on sloppy, slippery boards, he is trampled under the others' hoofs, and squeezed by their huge bodies, and suffocated by the pressure and foulness.

Through the livelong night, while we Christians on board are sleeping in our berths, these horrid scenes are enacted, and no one to see them. Morning comes, and the dead must be taken from the living. A great boom is rigged up, and as we lean over the rail to look on there is a chain let down, and the steam-winch winds and winds it tight and straining with some strong weight below, far, far down, in the lowest of the three tiers of "filet de bœuf," where no light enters, and whence a Stygian reeking comes.

Slowly there comes up first the black, frowning, murdered head and horns, and dull blue eyes and ghastly grinning face of a poor dead bullock, then his pendent legs and his huge long carcase.

To see the owner's mark on his back they scrape away the slush and grime, then he is swung over the sea, and a stroke of the axe cuts the rope round his horns. Down with a splash falls the vast heavy carcase; and £20 worth of meat floats on a wave or two, then it is engulfed. Another and another, and twenty-two are thus hauled up and cast into the sea, and this, too, on the first day of a very calm passage. What must it be in a storm? Oh, the roast beef of old England!

## END NOTES

1—An agitation on this subject has at last resulted in great amelioration of these miseries. The account of our passage in the Falke was published separately for this purpose, and had a wide circulation.

# CHAPTER XXIV.

The Cornwall — Running over a Steamer — Gushing —
Queen Elizabeth — The Last Peril — Road to Death —
Driven Mad — Touching Sight.

After two nights at sea, we sight the shores of Essex, and
fleets of full-sailed ships converging show us the mouth of
the mighty, wealth-bearing Thames. Here are five young
sailor-lads on our deck who are coming back to their homes
after a three years' cruise. They soon get fond of the crew of
the Rob Roy; and it is a good time to say words of warning,
of kindness, of encouragement, of home, of mothers, of
Bibles, of life and of death, of heaven and of Christ. It is our
last opportunity during this summer journey, and it is not
thrown away.

Thames Haven is about ten miles below Gravesend, and
when the steamer stops here the Rob Roy, impatient as to
waiting until all the live oxen are put ashore, slides over
into the water and up with the flag. Hurrah! we are
paddling again. Never was there a finer day for a canoe
than the 29th of September; and, on the rising tide, among a
whole crowd of ships, the little oaken argonaut cheerily flits
by. A Swedish barque passes, and I take hold of her for a
chat. Nay, she belongs to Mr. Dixon, of Sweden, and has
come straight from Stockholm, so the canoe is at once
recognized on board as an old friend. Paddling along then
to Purfleet, where I had been well pleased last year (resting

my first Sunday in the old Rob Roy), I came ashore, and the people ran out to meet me from the hotel; and the boys in the Reformatory school-ship Cornwall "manned" the bulwarks, and all gave a ringing cheer, for the captain of the canoe had paid them also a visit twelve months ago.

A good lunch was on board the Rob Roy in a few minutes, and she sped on and on, till, at a distance, I saw the funnel and masts of a great steamer, the Foyle, which had been sunk by a collision in the river, and we made straight for her midships; and though the men in boats around shouted to warn, and ordered to go back, the Rob Roy actually paddled right over her deck, with a powerful stream rushing and hissing through the rigging, and many tangled ropes all hanging about, exulting at last that she had certainly run over a steamer, though no steamer ever had run over her.

For a thousand miles and more she has carried me safely; and three hundred of this when sailing. Twenty-five steamers have borne us both for another good thousand miles on lake and sea and river, and for five hundred miles we have gone by rail. Yet here is the boat as stanch and straight, and almost as neat and polished as in hot July; and the crew, though bronzed and bearded, all perfectly well. Only two months, and only £50 have been spent on this most delightful cruise; and yet how many new incidents, thoughts, words, and deeds, have been graven in memory during that little time! I wonder myself at the complete success of the voyage; and I most thankfully acknowledged the continued blessings and goodness from on High that have followed it all through.

The log of my first canoe cruise may have appeared rather too enthusiastic in its expression of the delights of the paddle, but this would be excused because it was a first trip, and in a new way.

But matter-of-fact people will perhaps resent a second sentimental log, and expect that in a second voyage, just as on a second wedding-day, the "gushing" time is done.

Not so; for this northern cruise was even more enjoyable than the other, since I was more at ease in it, and had more confidence and comfort, and a better boat and more wind and more resources and more novelty of people and of scene. Perhaps, also, more danger; and now about this danger of canoeing let us say a word.

In the first place, in the canoe you endanger only yourself; no boatmen, no sailor-boy, no mountain-guides or porters, no climbing comrade, no Arab slave, no horse or mule, or ass even, except yourself. The lonely canoeist has the minimum of responsibility, while he has the maximum of capacity for enjoyment. To have another life in charge is a serious drawback on adventure.

In olden days, when the Lord Chancellor rode in state, and the Queen was behind him on a pillion, it must have doubled his anxiety and halved his enjoyment—even of a steady amble through the City—to think that if his palfrey shied Elizabeth might break her neck. To steer a sailing-boat when a lady is in it is a misery to me, not a pleasure. As for the captain of a Cunarder with three hundred souls on board, I wonder ever that he can laugh and talk and sleep with so many lives in keeping.

Some people think, however, that to risk even one's own life in a canoe is wrong; but surely this depends on *how much risk*. Every manly exercise has risk, with gun or rifle, horse or cricket-ball, running, climbing, skating, rowing, driving, boxing, fencing, wrestling, nay, even in fishing, and in the very walk of a "constitutional," you have risk of life and limb.

Nor is it only abroad and in desert places that exercise has most risk, though it may have most romance, and may sound, when told, as most full of danger.

In the home life of England, and in common days and places, we meet risk that must be encountered, but must not be narrated, just because it is common.

And yet we must now do this very thing, being forced to tell truly the last dangerous venture of our cruise, though it happened in England; for it is the law of all logs that no page may be omitted from their history.

Before reaching home to place the little Rob Roy on the writing-table where she now reclines, with sails all set and flag triumphant, but at rest, I had to cross one more stream, not broad but strong, and it was now most strong and dangerous.

Though its course was long, there was only one bridge over it, and this was old and steep, and, in fact, inaccessible, serving only to contract the channel, and to confuse its current in eddies and back-lashes round the piers of the arch. Here another powerful stream entered the first, and numerous smaller rivulets poured in on various sides; one of them running in an ancient course hard by an old palace of King Hal. It was dark when we came to the verge of the current. It was raining too, and the channel was swollen—how deep I could not say, but much deeper than usual. First we examined the conformation of the banks, and this was very curious. On each side was a narrow stratum of smooth stone, and above this rose, high on the right and left, steep, beetling cliffs of indurated clay, red and yellow and black, with vitrifactions at intervals, and here and there some wood.

The current flowed apace, and heaved up with violent surges, bearing along great logs of timber, piles of wicker work, carts and furniture, probably from distant villages, even small haystacks, and horses and dogs and other live animals. Sometimes, in such floods a whole herd of bullocks have been hurried past, noisily lowing in the dark, gusty night; but even now, when we came to it, the sounds and cries were most appalling of men and even women, carried by in crowds, some of them clinging desperately to the great piles of wood that seemed in the dusk like houses, with windows and doors looming high in the din and hurly-burly.

I cried aloud to one of these, which was covered to the roof with human beings; but the only answer to my hail was a wild shriek to shudder at—"Bankcity-bank!" he cried—the despairing wail of some poor hapless one, made maniac by his peril; and yet, to show how reckless men are, even in danger, there were two youths perched high on the crazy drifting roof, who quietly smoked their pipes while the great machine rolled from side to side, as if it would dash against the iron light-houses on the edge of the stream, or the cliffs of clay beyond.

For safety's sake men were stationed on the flat ledges by the channel below, as a sort of Coastguard, clad in blue, and wearing black helmets. They could readily tell us where was the best ford, but they could not aid us more.

There was no ferry-boat by which to cross this dreadful current; as for my canoe, it would have been madness to paddle here. How I wished to be safe in her again on the deepest part of Venern! Then I thought of getting a horse; but this was impossible. Yet cross the stream I must, and the only way left was to ford it on foot.

Experience gained in the other stormy days of the tour here came to my aid; and I looked about for some friendly island whereon to rest for a moment, even in mid stream, but none was near. Indeed, where these islands do occur (rarely enough in the 2000 miles of the current's course) they are often crowded by people, trembling and frightened, who can move neither back nor forward from fear—and well may they be afraid, for the impetuous torrent maims or slays outright 200 people every year.

By my side, then, I observed a band of little children, timidly clasping each others' tiny, cold, wet hands, and gazing on the fearful scene. One of these babes carried in her arms a still smaller babelet, also a jug of beer, a weekly newspaper, a pat of butter, and a red herring—a touching sight to see, while the rain poured ruthlessly, and the shouting of men and jingling of bells and splashing of water mingled with the roar of the dark, fast stream. Clutching my log for a life-buoy, and nerved for a desperate effort, I dashed in with a shout.

Aha! we have safely crossed the Strand; and here is the dark old bridge of

TEMPLE BAR.

# APPENDIX

# APPENDIX

(a) REMARKS on the management of a canoe, especially in currents, have been given at length in the Appendix of my former book; and it need only be said here that another year's experience confirms what has there been stated.

(b) Experiments as to the use of leeboards for improving the sailing qualities of a canoe have convinced me that a light leeboard of sheet-iron or of deal will be a useful addition to the gear

(c) For a long day's work, light shoes are very desirable in the canoe. The benefit of them in allowing full play to the feet is most remarkable. Of course, another pair of thick-soled shoes are absolutely necessary for rough work on shore.

(d) Wheels for transporting the canoe on land have been used with approval during some short voyages in England and on the Rhine. The wheels are about one foot in diameter, and with their fittings weigh from 6 lb. to 9 lb. But for a long voyage, where so great an addition to the cargo is a very serious matter, I should not think of carrying wheels. During two of my long trips the want of wheels was really felt only for one mile, and to carry 8 lb. weight for 1999 miles in order to use them for one, is not economical. On shore you should husband your strength by obtaining men to help; and in foreign lands you generally have one man in each town as a guide to the hotel. The safest place, too, for your boat in a crowded, narrow street is upon men's shoulders, and not among the legs of a dozen young urchins, and the wheels of carts. On the *portages* of the Vrangs Elv or the Danube, wheels would have been utterly useless, and only so many more pounds weight to carry through the thick forests or over the rocks. In my third Eastern cruise, I carried a small pair of wheels, only 2 lb. weight, for ten thousand miles—and never used them once!

(e) And here it may be mentioned that ladies, too, have taken to the paddle, and they seem to enjoy the pleasures of the canoe. It certainly is much easier for a lady to paddle than to pull two sculls in a rowing-boat; for there are no "crabs" to be caught in the canoe, and the fair canoeiste can always see where she is going, while she leans gracefully back on a cushion, and there is ample room in the "well" for the moderately profuse crinoline now in vogue.

N.B. — Ladies are eligible as honorary members of the Canoe Club; and it is to be remembered that two canoes paddling in company can keep much nearer together than two boats with oars.

(f) "Paddle your own canoe." The earliest claimant I can find for the use of these words in verse is Mr. George Wortabot, a Syrian gentleman whose MS. Bears date 1860. Those of us who have obeyed the injunction contained in that doggerel line will endorse the opinion of the paddler in Nottingham, who writes, "I have all the pleasure of a yacht without the expense."

## (B.) — DESCRIPTION OF THE ROB ROY.

AMONG the many who are building canoes, there may be some persons who have undue expectations as to what such boats can do. Now, the three kinds of canoes, for racing, for sailing, and for travelling, are quite distinct in their forms and capabilities.

A long, narrow, light racing-canoe, with a long-spooned paddle, will attain great speed.

A sailing-canoe with flat bearing, and some keel, will sail admirably.

The "travelling-canoe" has to sail, to paddle, and to bear portage and rough handling.

The endeavour to combine these three qualities in suitable proportions, without sacrificing more of any of them than can be well dispensed with, has led to the building of the canoe now to be described; and the new Rob Roy has been a great success.

The old Rob Roy canoe (of 1865), which made a voyage through France, Germany, &c., was specially built for the purpose; and it is described in the book which gives an account of that journey. A more detailed description was given in the Transactions of the Institute of Naval Architects, but the numerous improvements suggested during this voyage, and in careful experiments afterwards, were embodied in the new Rob Roy, which is now to be described, so that this novel, inexpensive, and healthful mode of travelling may be facilitated.

The Rob Roy was designed to sail steadily, to paddle easily, to float lightly, to turn readily, and to bear rough usage on stones and banks, and in carts, railways, and steamers; to be durable and dry, as well as comfortable and safe. To secure these objects every plank and timber was carefully considered beforehand, as to its size, shape, and material, and the result has been most successful.

In the efforts to obtain a suitable canoe for this purpose ready made, it was soon found that boat-builders might be proficient at the cabinet-makers' work of their calling, without any knowledge of the principles required for a new design, especially when sailing, paddling, and carrying had to be provided for at once; and the requirements for each were not understood, except by those who had personally observed them, and had known how to work the paddle as well as the saw and the plane.

A canoe ought to fit a man like a coat; and to secure this the measure of the man should be taken for his canoe. The first regulating standard is the length of the man's feet, which will determine the height of the canoe from keel to deck; next, the length of his leg, which governs the size of the "well;" and then the weight of the crew and luggage, which regulates the displacement to be provided for. The following description is for a canoe to be used by a man 6 feet high, 12 stone weight, and with boots 1 foot long in the sole.

The Rob Roy is built of the best oak, except the top streak of mahogany, and the deck of fine cedar. The weight, without fittings, is 60 lb., and with all complete 71 lb. Lightness is not of so much consequence in this case as good lines, for a light boat if crank, will tire the canoeist far more in a week's cruise than would a heavier but stiff craft, which does not strain his body at every moment to keep her poised under the alternate strokes of the paddle or the sudden pressure of a squall on the sail.

The illustration on the opposite page represents, on a scale of a quarter of an inch to the foot, fig. 1, a section, with masts and sails; fig. 2, a bird's eye view of the deck. The woodcuts at pages 220, 222 represent, on a scale of an inch to the foot, figs. 3 and 4, cross sections at the beam and at the stretcher; figs. 9, 10, and 11, the backboard and the apron; the rest of the drawings showing particular portions more minutely. The principal dimensions are: Length over all, A S, 14 feet; from stem to beam, B, 7 feet 6 inches; beam, outside (6 inches abaft midships) 26 inches; depth from top of deck at C, fore end of the well, to upper surface of keel, 11 inches; keel, depth outside, 1 inch, with an iron band along its whole length, 3/8 inch wide; camber, 1 inch; depth at gunwale, 8½ inches. The upper streak is of mahogany, and quite vertical at the beam, where its depth is 3 inches. The garboard streaks, and the next on each side are strong, while the next two on each side are light, as it is found that they are less exposed than the others, particularly in a canoe where all these lower streaks are of oak. The stem and stern posts project over deck, the canoe, if turned over, will rest

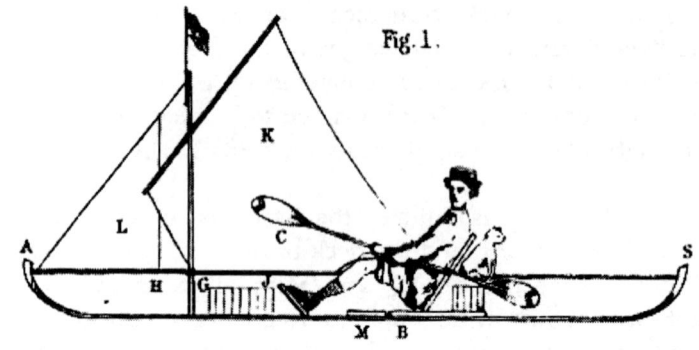

Fig. 1.

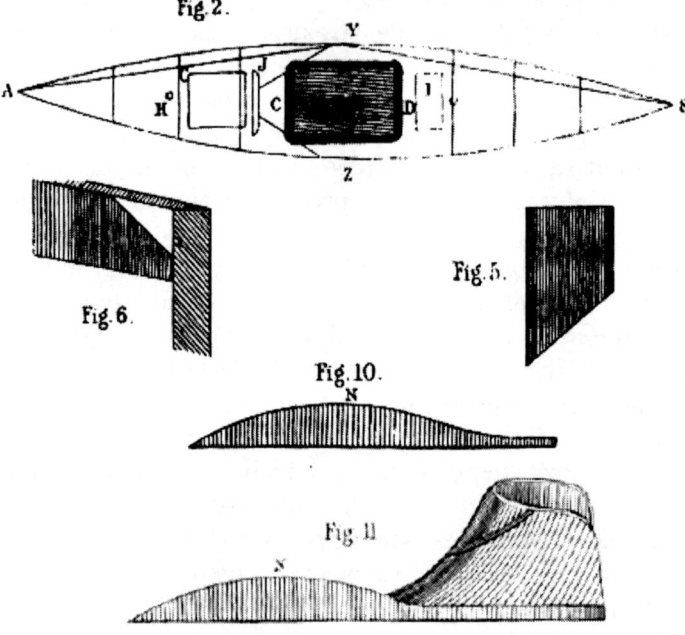

Fig. 2.

Fig. 6.

Fig. 5.

Fig. 10.

Fig. 11.

Scale of Figs 1 & 2, ⅛ of an inch to the foot.

on the upper edge of the combing, round the well, 1/8 inch deep, projecting ½ inch, of steamed oak, curved at the corners, and adding, by its angular position, very much to the strength of the deck about the well. The well is 32 inches from C to D, and 20 inches from E to F, so placed that D M is 2 feet, and thus the beam of the boat being aft of the midships the weight of the luggage, G, and of the masts and sails stowed forward, brings the boat to nearly an even keel. The additional basket of cooking-things at I (fig. 2) brings her a little by the stern. For a boat without luggage the beam should be 1 foot abaft midships to secure an even keel.

The deck is supported on four carlines forward and three aft, the latter portion being thus more strengthened, because, in some cases, it is required to support the weight of the canoeist sitting on the deck with his legs in the water. Each carline has a piece cut out of its end (see fig. 6), so that the water inside may run along the beam when the canoe is canted to sponge it out. The after edge of the carline at C is bevelled off (fig. 5 in section), so as not to catch the shins of your legs. All the carlines are narrow and deep, to economize strength, and the deck is screwed to them with brass screws, so that it might be removed for internal repairs. A flat piece is inserted under the deck at the mast-hole H, which is also furnished with a flanged brass ring. The deck is so arched as to enable the feet to rest comfortably on the broad stretcher J (fig. 4), the centre of it being cut down in a curve, in order that the mast and sails, rolled together, may rest there when there is no luggage, and be kept under the deck, but above any wet on the floor.[1] When there is luggage (as in this voyage) I usually put the mast and sails under the after deck. The cedar deck round the well at E F is firmly secured by knee-pieces, and the boat may thus be lifted up *by any part*, and may be sat upon *in any position* without injury. The luggage for three months, weighing 9 ½ lb., is carried in a black leather-cloth bag, 1 foot by 1 foot by 5 inches deep (G, figs. 1 and 2).

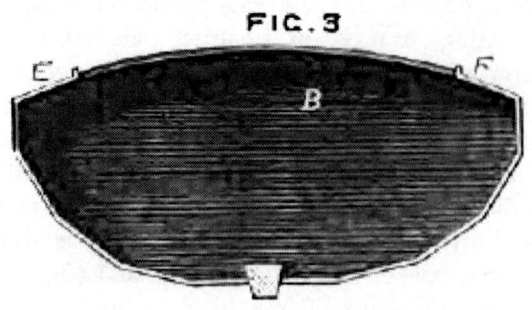

FIG. 3

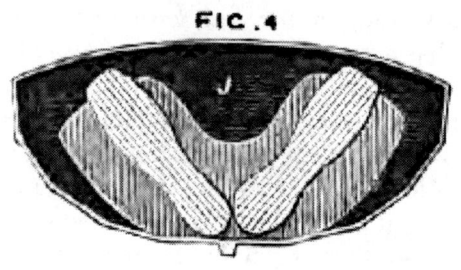

FIG. 4

FIG. 5

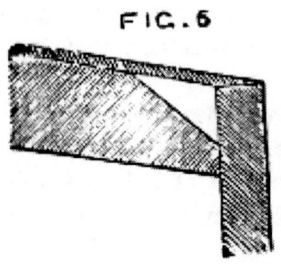

FIG. 6

A water-tight compartment may be made by an after bulkhead, with a lid to open, so as to allow the air to circulate when on shore.

The floor-boards, about 2 feet long, rest on the timbers until, at the part below C (fig. 2) they end at P P (fig. 7), in notched grooves, which fit into short oak pieces M N, ¼ inch thick, sloping forwards on each side of the keel O. Their ends rest on the garboard streaks, and so lower the heels nearly 1 inch below the level of the floor-board on the top of the timbers. The canoeist sits on the floor-boards. I prefer this to any cushion or mat whatever; but if a mat or cushion be used, it should be firmly fixed, especially in rough water. The canoeist's knees touch the combing and the apron boards, while his heels touch the keel. Thus the dotted lines in fig. 1, from the stretcher to the deck, show how the shin-bones are supported in comfort, enabling the paddler to sit for hours together without straining. But comfort is additionally secured by my new kind of backboard, shown in figs. 8 and 9, in section and elevation. This consists of two strips of oak, 18 inches long, 2 ½ inches wide, and united by a cross piece at Y, and another at X, the latter being grooved (fig. 8), so as to rest on the top of the combing, and to oscillate with the movement of the canoeist's back, which is thus supported on both sides along the muscles, while the spine is untouched between the strips. The dotted line U, (fig. 8) is a strong cord passed round all (through a hole in the deck or two eyes), and this serves to keep the backboard in general upright, while it is free to vibrate, or when on shore, to be closed down flat on deck or to be removed entirely in a moment by unloosing the cord. The use of this backboard is a leading feature of the canoe, and adds very much indeed to the canoeist's comfort, and, therefore, to his efficiency. The length and width of the oaken strips, and the width of the interval between them, ought to be carefully adjusted to the size and

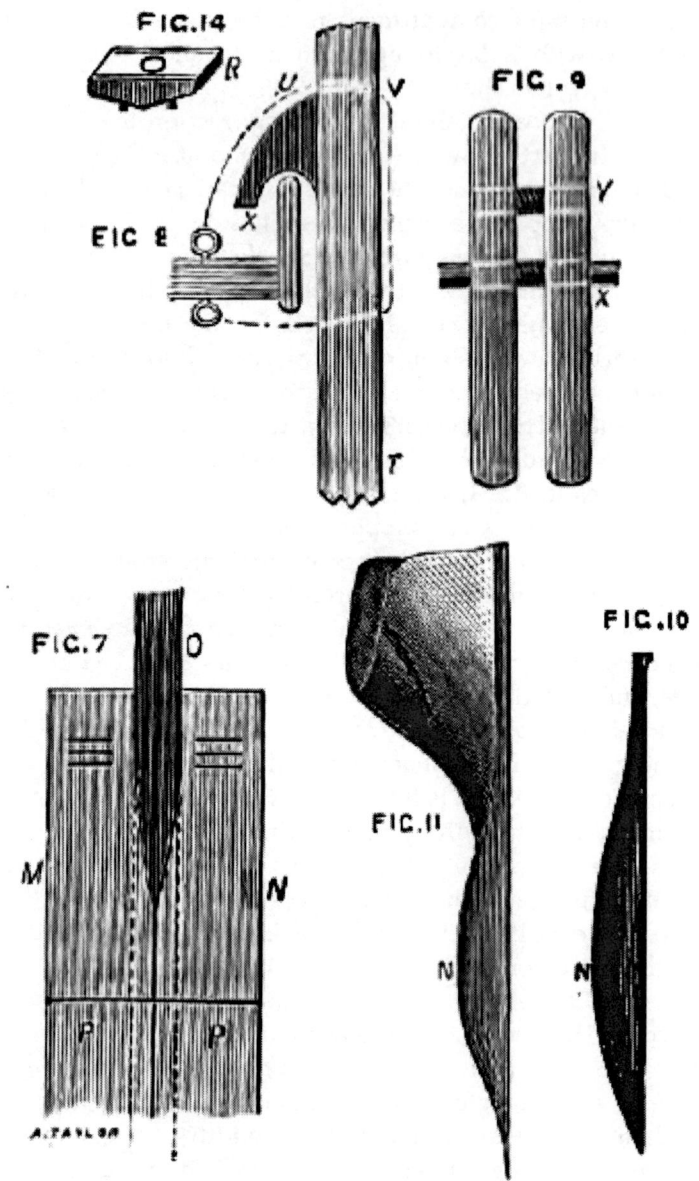

FIG.14

FIG.9

FIG.8

FIG.7

FIG.11

FIG.10

A.TAYLOR

224

"build" of the canoeist, just as a saddle ought to fit a horse, and its rider too.

The paddle is 7 feet long, flat-bladed, with a breadth of 6 inches in each palm, which is copper-banded, and made of the best spruce fir, the weight being little over 2 lb.[2] The spoon-shaped blade is better for speed, and a longer paddle is suitable for a racing-boat, but for a travelling canoe, where long paddling, occasional sailing, and frequent "shoving," require the instrument to combine lightness, straight edge, handiness, and strength, it is found that a short paddle is best for the varied work of a protracted voyage. Leather cups have been usually employed on the wrists of the paddle to catch the dripping water, but round india-rubber rings look much better and answer every purpose, if placed just above the points where the paddle dips into the water in an ordinary stoke. The rings may be had for two-pence, and can be slipped on over the broad blade. If necessary, two are used on each side, and they bear rough usage well, while if they strike the cedar deck, no injury is done to it.

After numerous experiments, the following very simple plan has been devised for a waterproof apron, and its application at once removes one of the chief objections to canoes in rough water, as heretofore constructed. It is necessary to have a covering for the well which shall effectually exclude the water, and yet be so attached as not to hamper the canoeist in case of an upset, or when he desires to get out of the boat in a more legitimate manner. These desiderata are completely secured by the new apron, which is not permanently attached in any manner to the boat, but is formed as follows: a piece of light wood, of the form in fig.10, 2 feet long and 3 inches deep at the deepest part, is placed along each side of the deck vertically, so as just to rest against the outside of each knee of the canoeist, and then a piece of macintosh cloth (drab colour is best) is tightly nailed along and over these, so as to form an apron, supported at each side on Z (fig. 11), and sloping from the highest part forwards down to the deck in front of the combing, over which its edge projects 1 inch, and then lies flat. The other or after end is so cut and formed as to fit the body neatly, and the ends may be tucked in behind, or, when the waves are very rough, they should be secured *outside* the backboard by a string with a knot, When this apron is so applied, and the knees are in position, their pressure keeps the whole apron steady, and the splash of small waves is not enough to move it. In rough water I place a string across the end and round two screw nails on the deck; or an india-rubber cord run through the hemmed end, but best of all is a strip of wood bent across the deck with its ends under two screws or chocks.

A button-hole at the highest point of the apron, allows it to be supported on the waistcoat. When you have to get out on shore, or when sailing, it is usually best to stow the apron away, so that the legs may be turned into any desired position of ease. The apron I used in this tour had been perfectly fitted by myself to me and the boat. Several others, a little like it, (very little!) roughly made for other canoes, have, as might be expected, failed to give satisfaction.[3]

One important advantage of a canoe is the capacity for sailing without altering the canoeist's seat; and we shall no describe the mast and sails found by experience to be the most convenient, after three masts had been broken and eight sets of sails had more or less failed. The mast is 1 ¾ inches thick (tapering), and 5 feet 6 inches long, of which the part above deck is 4 feet 9 inches. The lug-sail K (fig. 1), has a yard and a boom, each 4 feet 9 inches long, so that when furled the end of the boom and mast come together. The fore-leach is 2 feet long, and the after-leach 6 feet six inches, giving an area of about 15 square feet. The yard and boom are of bamboo, and the yard passes into a broad hem on the sail-head, while the halyard is rove aloft through a small boxwood block ¾ inch long, and with a brass sheave, and through another (a brass blind pulley) well fastened on the side of the mast near the deck, so that the sail can be lowered and hoisted readily. The lower joint of a fishing-rod, 4 feet 9 inches long, is a spare boom. The tack end of the boom is made fast to the mast by a flat piece of leather, lashed to its upper part and to the mast, and so as to be free to swing in every direction; after many other plans had failed this was quite successful, and lasted through the whole voyage. No hole is made in the mast, and no nail or screw driven into it, for these are causes of weakness. Two cord loops, about 6 inches apart, near the mast-head, support the flagstaff, of bamboo-cane 2 feet long, and with a silk flag 7 inches by 9 inches. When the mast is not used this flagstaff is detached and placed in the mast-hole, which it fits by a button 2 inches wide, permanently fixed on the staff, the lower end of which rests in the mast-step. The halyard and sheet should be of woven cord, which does not untwist, and is soft to handle in the wet. The sheet when not in hand may be belayed round a cleat on deck on either side of the apron, where it is highest, and thus these cleats are protected from the paddle.

For the sake of convenience the mast is stepped so far forward as to allow the boom to swing past the canoeist's breast when the sail is jibbed or brought over. This also allows the luggage-bag to be between the stretcher and the mast. Thus the mast-hole H is a 3 feet 6 inches' distance from the stem. The mast-step is a simple wedge-like piece of oak (see R, fig. 14), made fast to the keel, and abutting on the garboard streak on each side, with a square hole in it for the foot of the mast. It may be thought that the mast is thus stepped too far forward, but the importance of having the sail free to swing, without lying against the canoeist's body, or getting entangled with his paddle, which is used in steering, is so great, that some sacrifice must be made to secure this point. However, it is found that the boat sails very well on a wind with this sail, if the breeze is strong;

and in light breezes it is only expedient to sail with the wind well aft, when the jib can also be used. A canoe must have a strong, light, flexible painter, suitable for constant use, because a great deal has to be done by its means in towing on dull water, guiding the boat while wading down shallows or beside falls, lowering into locks, hauling her over hedges, wall, locks, banks, and even houses; and raising or lowering her (with luggage in) to and from steamboats. The "Alpine Club" rope, used in the new Rob Roy, was found to be hard and "kinky" when wet, and the softer rope used in the old Rob Roy was far better. Another kind of brown-tanned rope has been recommended. The painter should not be longer than twice the length of the boat. Each end is whipped with wax-end, which sort of fine twine is also invaluable for all the other fastenings, as it never slips. The painter passes through a hole in the stem, and another in the stern-post, and is drawn tight to lie on deck in the lines A Y and S Y, fig. 2; the slack of about four feet is belayed round the windward cleat and coiled outside, so that it may be seized instantly when you go ashore, or have to jump out to save a smash or an overset in a dangerous place. This mode of fixing and belaying the painter I adopted after numerous trials of other plans, and it is found to be far the best.

The jib is a triangle of 3 feet hoist and 3 feet foot, the fore-leach fast by a loop, passing under the painter and over the stem; the head is fixed by a loop over the mast-head, and under the flagstaff button. Thus the jib can be struck while the canoeist remains in the boat, by pushing off these two loops with his paddle. To set the jib, it is best to land. This is much more generally convenient than to have jib-tackle on the mast. (I have now discarded the jib entirely.) The sails are of calico, without any seam. This lasts quite well enough, dries speedily, and sets well, too, provided that care is taken to have it cut out with the sevage along the after-leach, and not along any of the other sides.

Inattention to this last direction simply ruins sails; and it cannot be too often repeated that the success of the six Rob Roy voyages could not be expected if great care had not been devoted to all these details.

A good travelling canoe, costing £15, ought to last a long time, for it is not racked and pulled in piece at every stroke, as a rowing boat is. We have more than 200 canoes in the Canoe Club.

END NOTES

1—The Jordan canoe had many improvements which are explained in the Jordan book. The stretcher is in two separate pieces, abutting on the carline above, and thus exceedingly light and strong, and easily moveable.

2—The paddle of an Esquimaux kyak lately examined, was 6 feet 11 inches long and 5 ½ inches broad in the palm, and the ends had the corners rounded off. The Esquimaux use a piece of fish-skin wound spirally along the paddle, in place of the rings above mentioned. The paddle of the Norway cruise went also on the Jordan and another voyage besides.

3—The "apron" of the Jordan Rob Roy was different in construction as explained in "The Rob Roy on the Jordan." It has a short six-inch hatch of arched wood, and a light cane arched over the knees, which answers perfectly. Five years ago I discarded the long wooden hatch.

## (C.)—DANISH MISSIONS.

THE following particulars are taken chiefly from "Denmark and her Missions," the book already referred to in the text :

Christianity was introduced into Denmark in the ninth century. Harold was the first king who openly professed it. Many English names come from Denmark.

All our cinque ports have names of Scandinavian origin; and the name of Havelock is enshrined in a strange old story of the twelfth century. The incident about Canute and the tide reminds us that, there being no ebb and flow in the Baltic, the courtiers would naturally have their attention drawn to the rising tide in England.

In the royal library at Copenhagen I saw the old MS. of part of the Old Testament in Danish, written in the fourteenth century, on goat skins dyed red. In 1515 Peterson, and in 1524, Mikkelsen gave a complete Danish translation of the whole Bible, which appeared two years before Tyndale's English New Testament in our own country; but it was not published as a whole until 1556, under Christian III. In the seventeenth century, Frederick IV., a great Danish monarch, made fresh efforts to circulate the Bible in his territory. He used to read several chapters every day, and his influence extended for many years in this important matter.

Viborg was the first Protestant town. In 1688 each church had a "Kirke Gubbe," or "church pusher," whose duty it was to wake up sleepers; while an hour-glass placed on the pulpit told the preacher he must not speak too long.

Numerous family ties have united the royal families of England and Denmark from the time when Gorme, a Danish king, 1000 years ago, married Thyra, daughter of Ethelred, king of England.

The Scotchmen Henderson and Patterson, in 1805 commenced a Bible Society in Denmark. The grandson of George II. of England became its president, and used to preach from selected texts. Various persons of distinction aided these efforts in more modern times; and now there is a regular agency for Bible distribution, and for the circulation of tracts among all classes of the people.

But it is especially in the foreign missionary field that the early, active, and successful exertions of the Danes deserve to be recorded. They were, in many cases, the pioneers of the church, and laboured out a way for the Gospel through endless obstacles, and in dark and weary days, when man did little to help and much to hinder. A few of their splendid achievements in this grand battle of the Cross may be briefly noticed, even while we pause in our journey to gaze back into past centuries.

With respect, then, first, to the mission work in India; we may pass over the labours of Xavier, as their true character has been exposed on examination; and, like other Popish conversions, nearly all the alleged instances of it seem to have been merely external changes of form, and not internal conversion of heart; and the Jesuits themselves allow that their mission efforts at that time ended in failure.

Frederick IV. of Denmark aided Ziegenbalch and Plutscho to go as missionaries, in 1705, to Tranquebar, and their work was helped by the Society for the Propagation of the Gospel in Foreign Parts, which had been set on foot four years previously; and by the Christian Knowledge Society, established two years before that. The King began a missionary college at Copenhagen. War forced the missionaries to go to Calcutta, where they soon began to preach, and were protected by Lord Clive; but the East India Company resolutely strove to debar all Christians from work of this sort; and it was only by claiming protection under the Danish flag that English Christians were allowed to proclaim the Gospel in a British possession. The first English missionary to India was the Rev. A. Clarke, in 1789. In 1814 Tranquebar was sold to England by the Danes, and the mission property was then transferred to a Saxon society.

At Tanjore, a native prince introduced the Gospel in 1722; and then came the great Swartz, who, with the aid of Colonel Wood, the conqueror of Hyder Ali, erected a church and school at Trichinopoli. He obtained great influence over the heathen princes, and died after long service, and after he had given much money to the missionary cause. One missionary, Dr. Eottler, laboured for sixty years. William Carey, a cobbler, determined to become a missionary to the Hindoos; and, being refused a passage in the East India Company's ships, he appealed to a Dane, who took him out willingly, with his family, to Serampore, a Danish colony, where the mission was firmly established; and Carey died in old age, after building a college on the Hooghly for 450 missionary students, which was endowed and protected by the King of Denmark, and was specially provided for when Serampore was transferred to England in 1845. Marshman, Judson, and Henry Martyn were aided in their work from hence; and an unsuccessful effort was made to establish a station in Bhootan, where so much trouble has been caused within the last few years to British interests.

Sixty years ago, Taylor was sent by the Church Missionary Society to Bombay, under Danish protection; the East India Company being still bitterly hostile to the truth.

Turning now to Greenland, we find that in A.D. 1023 it became tributary to Norway; but for a long time the place was forgotten, until Frederick IV., instigated by Hans Egede, established a mission station there, after repeated failures, shipwrecks, and famines, in 1721; and the work being continued by Stach and Count Zinzendorf, the Moravians took up the mission, and zealously laboured for years with most wonderful perseverance, and amid dangers and difficulties quite appalling.

In the West Indies, also, the Danes were moved to preach Christ to the wretched slaves in their settlements; and Dober began, in 1732, at the island of St. Thomas, amid dreadful privations and discouragements; but the persecution by the Governor was mitigated through the intervention of the good Count Zinzendorf; and, in twenty years, Christian teachers were even sought for by many of the planters.

F. Martin preached in St. Jan, and others at St. Croce; until from these Danish islands the Gospel was first sounded forth to the people of Jamaica, Antigua, St. Kitts, Barbadoes, and Tobago. The Church of the United Brethren has 314 missionaries in foreign lands, with 80,000 people under their charge, and 200 schools—their heathen congregations being about four times as great as their own number at home.

**Want to build your own Rob Roy?**
**Here's some additional help...**

*Practical Boat Building for Amateurs*
Adrian Neison, Dixon Kemp

ISBN-10: 1-929516-13-4
ISBN-13: 978-1-929516-13-1
$ 9.99

Learn more at:

www.dixonprice.com

Lightning Source UK Ltd.
Milton Keynes UK
07 September 2010
159522UK00001B/15/P